# America's Quest for Peace

# DEXTER PERKINS

# America's
# Quest for Peace

*Indiana University Press ~ Bloomington*

Chapter 3 is adapted by permission from an article which
appeared in the Virginia Quarterly Review, Autumn 1960

Manufactured in the United States of America

Library of Congress catalog card number: 61-13718

327.73
P

# Contents

# Preface

THE THREE LECTURES WHICH I HAD THE privilege of giving at the University of Virginia under the James W. Richard lectureship in 1959 deal with a vast subject. Volume on volume might be written on the problem with which they deal. My purpose has been a limited one. It is to detach from the complicated story some of the most meaningful generalizations that can be derived from it. In this attempt I hope I have succeeded. The lectures have been revised and brought up to date for publication in book form.

I take this occasion to thank my Virginia friends for the friendly reception they accorded me, and especially to thank Professor Richard Henneman and Professor Edward Younger for the opportunity they afforded me to talk on a subject close to my heart, and the long-time concern of my studies.

DEXTER PERKINS

*Rochester, New York*
*March, 1961*

# ~< 1 >~

# Peace through Law

THE HISTORY OF MAN IS A HISTORY OF violence. From the dawn of civilization to the present time, states have risen and fallen, always through struggle and war. Our own nation came into being through war and was preserved from dissolution in another war. Twice in the last half century the United States has been involved in struggles of the fiercest character. Yet side by side with this, there has always existed here in America a desire that things should be otherwise; there have always been statesmen to exalt peace. "There never was a good war, or a bad peace," said Benjamin Franklin. "Peace is our passion," said Thomas Jeffer-

[9]

son. In the First World War, Woodrow Wilson pled in moving words for a new international order. In the speech of the four freedoms, Franklin Roosevelt placed first in the list freedom from war. All over this broad land today men hunger for peace. How are they to find it? It is certain that the search will be difficult; it is by no means certain that it will be successful. Yet it is safe to say that the need to examine the problem has never been greater than it is today, at a time when the agencies of destruction have grown so portentously, and when the consequences of war on the grand scale might be little less than mutual annihilation. In so examining it, we can measure more accurately the possibilities by looking at the record. We can avoid previous errors, if we review the story. We can gain a new sense of proportion as to what is involved. In this book I propose to examine the American attitude toward the quest for peace, and try to see what it teaches us as to the world and the period in which we live. I shall consider three main approaches: peace through law, peace through collective security, and peace through the reduction of armaments.

In no country has the great question of the elimination of war aroused a more active interest than in the United States. Looking at the matter historically, the earliest recipe prescribed to deal with it is the fortification and extension of international law. The subject of international law played an increasing part in college curricula in the years at the turn of the century. The feeling was growing that here was a way to deal effectively with the vexing questions of international intercourse, and that with the extension of legal principles international strife might be, if not averted, at least made much less likely.

It is not strange that such a development took place. The United States itself came into being through a written constitution which exalts the reign of law; a deep respect for legal process exists in the American character, even though there are times when it dissolves under severe strain; the nation is largely ruled by lawyers who find it easy to believe that what works in a civil society will work in the society of nations; what is more logical than to substitute for caprice and violence a set of fixed, yet evolving, rules to govern the intercourse of nations?

As a matter of fact, though many people do not realize the fact, there has been a substantial growth of international law in the last hundred years, and still more in the last fifty years. There are cynics who will tell you that there is no such thing as international law. Of course these people are wrong. There are widely accepted principles of international intercourse, and there is a vast body of treaties which are in essence legal documents governing the relations of the signatories to one another. Some of these treaties are truly international agreements, such, for example, as the Charter of the United Nations, or the Protocol creating the International Court of Justice; some are more restricted in their scope; but all of them are drafted in legal terms and all of them are subject to legal interpretation. There is not a foreign office in the world which does not employ specialists in the legal field in connection with its operations. It is foolish to say that international law is a mere figment of the imagination. It is equally foolish, I should observe, to say that its rules are constantly broken. As a matter of fact, within a wide area they are observed with as much regularity as the rules of municipal law; and when they are broken, the attempt is usually made to justify the breach on some legal ground.

But at the same time, experience does not suggest that the growth of legal principles has brought about a peaceful world, or prevented the outbreak of conflicts of large dimensions. In the last fifty years we have witnessed two colossal struggles, involving millions of lives and billions of treasure. Clearly the development of international law has not been adequate to restrain the forces of violence.

There are reasons why this is so. One of the reasons lies in the limited scope of the rules of law accepted by the international community. These rules are nothing like as extensive as the rules that govern the relations of individuals in a civil society. They leave a great many of the key problems of international intercourse untouched.

Why not extend them? The process is difficult. There exists no international legislature, nor, if I read the signs aright, no probability that such a legislature will come into existence. Only a tiny minority of persons, I believe, would question this view. It is, of course, possible at least in theory to bring about an extension of law through an international conference, which will draft agreements for ratification by the whole body of civilized states. But the past record does not suggest that a great deal can be done by these means. There has existed for some time a movement for codification of international law. In 1930 the League of Nations promoted a conference to advance this worthy cause. There were chosen for discussion three areas, in which it was thought to be easiest to arrive at a consensus, the international law of nationality, of territorial waters, and of state responsibility. Professor Morgenthau, in his *Politics Among the Nations,* sums up the result.

The conference was unable to reach any agreement with respect to territorial waters and state responsibility, and it could do no more than draft four conventions dealing with certain limited aspects of the international law of nationality. Even these conventions, which far from codify the whole international law of nationality, have been ratified by only ten states and hardly deserve to be called codifications in the sense in which the term is generally used. The spectacular failure not only demonstrates the inherent weakness of international law from the legislative point of view, but the fear of governments to compromise their national interests in some unforeseen way by agreeing to a certain rule of international law or a certain interpretation of an already recognized rule which may raise doubts as to the future.

The process of codification may well be more difficult today than it would have been fifty years ago. The rules of international law developed in the society of the West. They were shaped in the crucible of Western experience, and behind them lay generally accepted assumptions as to the nature of international society. Can they now be applied to new nations and governments which start with a different set of ideological assumptions, and which were not consulted when these rules were framed? Will not some of these new nations, which are loath to recognize the intellectual and moral leadership of the West, find it difficult to accept the principles which the West has defined? Will not the Communist-oriented nations, with their view of the future, find it difficult to construe international law in the same terms as the democracies? These are not idle questions, and they go to the root of the problem of the advancement of the law by the process of codification.

There is another way in which the law might grow. It might grow as the common law has grown, through the decisions of an international court, or a series of international courts. But here a difficulty at once arises. The great nations of the world, even the nations of the West, have shown a very limited disposition to submit their disputes to an international tribunal. There is nothing strange about this. In international adjudication, there are lacking some of the assurances that exist in the case of adjudication before national tribunals. In the latter case, it is possible to define the principles governing a given situation, if not perfectly, at least with a good deal more precision than in an international controversy. It is possible to have the case considered by regularly established tribunals, construing statutes and constitutions, and organized in a judicial hierarchy, and in general both parties to the dispute will acquiesce in the ultimate decision, and will, within limits, have the machinery to enforce it. None of these factors exists in the same sense in the field of international law. In major disputes there may not be any real legal principle to apply. There is an International Court of Justice, but no hierarchy of courts. The International Court has no power to enforce its decisions. Taking all these facts together, it is clear that the possibility of settling serious controversies by adjudication is limited.

But the difficulty lies deeper still. It lies in the fact that states have never admitted, and do not now admit, that their activities and relations with other states are inevitably controlled by legal principles. The notion of submission to law runs counter to the notion that each state is sovereign. States traditionally treat many matters which have international repercussions as if they were matters of purely domestic concern. They make laws affecting immigration, or trade, or naturalization, to take only some obvious examples, without feeling bound to consult the interest of any other state.

One may go still further. Even in civil society there are questions that cut so deep that a legal prescription will not solve them, questions which can be settled only by negotiation and adjustment, or by some kind of appeal to coercion. It would, for example, probably be impossible to draw up a code for the relations of capital and labor that would prevent strikes. An industrial controversy often involves an alteration of the *status quo,* and in such circumstances an appeal to a legal principle may prove inadequate. To take a still more serious case, it is possible that a domestic question will involve so drastic a change in the existing order as to be impossible of settlement under the forms of law. Such was the case with regard to the nature of our Federal Union, and as to the policy of the federal government with regard to slavery. An appeal had to be made to the sword.

Issues such as these, involving strong differences of opinion, and an appeal to emotions, occur far more often in the international than in the domestic sphere. And though there is, I believe, an increasing feeling that an appeal to violence is not the proper way to resolve them, historically violence has been frequently resorted to, and still more frequently threatened. In the absence of an international authority strong enough to keep the peace, the temptation has been to appeal to the right of the strong.

The general considerations I have been raising with regard to the inadequacy of international law as a guarantee of peace will, I fear, be given increased force if we examine the actual record so far as the United States is concerned. In no country has there been more discussion on the subject but if we get down to cases and to concrete steps to realize the ideal, we shall not find a great deal about which to cheer. Let us look, first, at the record of the United States with regard to the arbitration of international disputes; second, at the position of the United States with regard to the establishment of an international tribunal of wide competence and substantial prestige; third, at the major efforts of the American government to erect legal safeguards against war through engagements to submit disputes to a process of conciliation, or through a wide commitment not to resort to force; and fourth, at the attempt of the American government to lessen the possibility of war by domestic legislation intended to place restraints on the executive power, and to avoid involvement in international conflict.

First, let us look at the question of arbitration. Arbitration is a semi-judicial process. It involves the presentation of legal arguments, the preparation of legal briefs, the examination of these arguments and briefs before an impartial tribunal and the giving of a decision which is based upon the evidence. In the early days of American history, the United States undeniably accepted arbitration to a notable degree. Our first important treaty with Great Britain (after the peace treaty) provided for the arbitration of a whole variety of disputes. Much of our boundary with Canada has at one time or another been submitted to arbitration. In the period just after the Civil War we submitted to arbitration a highly important question, the question of the *Alabama* claims, arising out of the failure of Great Britain to prevent the construction in its own territory, and the departure therefrom, of a Confederate raider which worked severe damage upon the commerce of the United States. We arbitrated a sharp clash of views with Great Britain in 1895 as to the boundary between Venezuela and British Guiana. Nor were all our arbitrations with Great Britain. There are a substantial number of cases involving other powers. If one were to take the record down to the First World War it would seem to be an outstanding one.

Yet the melancholy fact is that in the last forty years the enthusiasm of the United States for arbitration seems to have declined. True, the claims of the American government for damages against Germany for the loss of American lives and property through the submarine warfare came before claims tribunals and two arbitral bodies decided a whole variety of controversies between Mexico and the United States. But the American record for the last thirty years is much less conspicuous than it was in the earlier period.

What is much more important is this. For the last sixty years the Senate of the United States has persistently refused to agree to any general arbitration agreement, that is, to any agreement which attempts to segregate certain classes of cases and bind the signatories

[19]

in advance to submit these cases to an arbitral tribunal. The record in this regard should be reviewed.

The Venezuela dispute of 1895, already alluded to, produced, first, a war scare, and second, a profound revulsion against the whole idea of armed conflict between the United States and Great Britain. The result was a treaty negotiated by the Cleveland administration which went further than any previous agreement signed by the United States. It provided that all "pecuniary claims" and "all other matters in difference, in respect of which either of the high contracting parties shall have rights against the other," should be submitted to arbitration, provided that such matters did not involve "the determination of territorial claims" or "the decision of a disputed question of principle of grave general importance" "affecting national rights." In these two reserved classes of cases, however, arbitration was still to take effect, except that an award was not to be binding if more than one member of a panel of six (three from each party) dissented. The agreement thus arrived at was submitted to the Senate of the United States in January of 1897.

And now, as was to be the case many times in the course of the next two decades, trouble began. In the Senate the treaty was roughly handled. Pursuing a course of action which was to make a mockery of every treaty of general arbitration, the Senate amended the draft submitted to it in a way that was almost lethal; it provided that no difference should be submitted which affected the honor, territorial integrity, or foreign or domestic policy of the United States; it barred any question involving a claim against any state and any question involving a judgment as to the continued existence of any agreement; and, worse than this, it stipulated that any specific question could be arbitrated only with the consent of two-thirds of the Senate, and that no question which any of the arbitrators in a given case deemed to be one of "grave general importance" should be further discussed. It would have been difficult to go further in limiting the usefulness of the structure so painfully reared by the British and American negotiators. But even after all these mutilations the Senate refused to advise and consent. The final vote was 43 in favor and 26 against, and thus the treaty died.

In 1904 President Theodore Roosevelt negotiated a series of treaties of arbitration with individual states which, by excluding all questions affecting "the vital interests, the independence, or the honor of the contracting states" certainly represented a very modest advance indeed. Nevertheless, the Senate treated them as it had the treaties of 1897. It appended a reservation to the effect that in each individual case a special agreement should be drawn up, and that this special agreement should require the consent of the Senate. The President was thoroughly disgusted with this action. He declared that the Senate reservation made the treaties shams. "My impression is," he wrote to Senator Lodge, "that we had better abandon the whole business rather than give the impression of trickiness and insincerity which would be produced by solemnly promulgating a sham." But, as in some other matters, Theodore Roosevelt, after marching gallantly up the hill, marched down again. In 1908, three years later, he consented to treaties which explicitly accepted the Senate point of view and in which was specifically incorporated a provision for a separate agreement on each matter to be arbitrated.

Hope springs eternal in the human breast. The Taft administration, under pressure of the peace societies and acting also, no doubt, from sincere conviction, attempted to approach the question of arbitration from another point of view. It promoted a series of agreements by which all justiciable questions should be arbitrated, and by which the question of whether a question was justiciable or not should be submitted to a board of inquiry. If the board of inquiry agreed, or if all but one of its members agreed, that the dispute was arbitrable, arbitration should take effect forthwith.

These agreements were the subject of a vigorous campaign by the President. He made speech after speech in their favor. But the Senate proceeded to mutilate them. It tacked on a reservation which excluded all sorts of questions—questions of immigration, questions of claims against the states of the Union, and of course questions involving that nebulous but widely accepted principle known as the Monroe Doctrine. Once more, having marched up the hill, the President of the United States was obliged to walk down again and the treaties had to be abandoned.

In 1928 the State Department came forward with a new formula, which provided that all differences relating to international matters involving a claim of right which had not been settled in any other way should be referred to arbitration. Mindful of previous experience, it excluded from arbitration matters which concern the domestic jurisdiction of either of the High Contracting Parties, matters involving the interest of third parties, matters involving the traditional attitude of the United States concerning American questions, and matters involving the obligations of other states under the Covenant of the League. It will be observed without much difficulty that the exceptions are more important than the inclusions, and that in effect the State Department capitulated to the Senate in advance.

It is not possible, therefore, to rejoice excessively that these treaties were approved.

There has been, then, a consistent reluctance on the part of the Senate of the United States to subscribe to meaningful generalized agreement for the arbitration of international disputes. But let us not take it out on the Senators. Had there existed among the American people as a whole an ardent or widespread support for such agreements, it is likely that they could have been drawn up and ratified. The plain fact of the matter is that the American public has never cared enough about international arbitration to generate powerful pressure in its favor and in this respect it is no different from the public of any other nation that I can think of. We are not likely to find peace along this road.

There are those who would say that the explanation of the reluctance to subscribe to some general formula for the arbitration of international disputes is due to the nature of international law, to its vagueness and its *lacunae*. Were there a reliable international body to construe the law, it might be argued, the situation would be different. But experience suggests the contrary. Since 1920 there has been such a body in the International Court of Justice loosely described as the World Court. Let us see what the history of the American attitude toward this Court reveals.

Down to 1919 it had not been possible to agree upon the constitution of an international tribunal which might hear cases in dispute with genuine authority. Contemporaneously, however, with the drafting of the Covenant, a committee of jurists, on which the United States was represented, hit upon an ingenious scheme to avoid the difficulties that had been previously raised by the rivalry of the large states and the small ones. This committee recommended that the judges of such a court would be elected, after nomination from the Hague lists, by the action both of the League Assembly, in which most of the states of the world were represented, and of the Council, in which the large states would have the principal voice. This expedient made possible the drafting of a protocol and the actual constitution, for the first time in history, of an international tribunal with widely recognized prestige. The United States actually participated in the nomination of candidates for election as judges, though it had not subscribed to the Covenant of the League of Nations.

In 1923 President Harding went further. He suggested to the Senate of the United States adhesion to the protocol creating the Court, with reservations making clear that the American government undertook no obligation under the Covenant itself. The proposal for American adhesion was endorsed by both political parties in the nominating conventions of 1924. It was also endorsed by a resolution passed by the House of Representatives. It was endorsed by President Coolidge. But when after nearly three years' delay the Senate finally got around to considering adhesion, it succumbed to its habit of making reservations. The World Court, under the statute creating it, had the right to issue advisory opinions. To some Senators this seemed a great and ominous threat to the position of the United States. Accordingly, it was stipulated in the vote of adhesion that the Court

should not render any advisory opinion except publicly and after due notice to all states adhering to the Court and to all interested states and after public hearing or opportunity for hearing given to any state concerned; nor shall it, without the consent of the United States, entertain any request for an advisory opinion touching any dispute or question in which the United States has or claims an interest.

It is not perhaps strange that the numerous signatories to the protocol had some difficulty in accepting this provision and it took years of discussion to formulate a proposal to overcome the obstacle. Finally, a commission of jurists drew up a new protocol in 1929 which went far to meet the objections of the Senate. It provided for consultation with the United States if the Court were asked for an advisory opinion, and permitted the United States to withdraw its support if its advice was not heeded. This new protocol was submitted to the Senate by President Hoover in December, 1930. This time years of delay ensued. Both political parties endorsed the plan in their platforms of 1932. The House of Representatives again expressed its sympathy with the objective. In 1935, later than seems to have been necessary, President Roosevelt requested the Senate to ratify the revised protocol.

One would hardly have thought that this request would have caused any very great political turmoil. The Court was a court of voluntary jurisdiction and therefore the United States could not be haled before it without its own consent. Yet when the Senate came to consider the protocol, a veritable flood of messages descended upon it. The Hearst papers formed the vanguard of the army of protest; the radio priest Father Coughlin, then at the height of his power, fulminated against the Court; the Senate was swamped by letters and telegrams of protest and at the final vote it rejected the new protocol by a vote of 53 to 37. Once again the project was shelved.

This is not quite the end of the story of the World Court. When the Charter of the United Nations was drafted in 1945, it contained provision for a Court of International Justice, not unlike the old World Court (which had expired with the League). In ratifying the Charter the United States gave its approval to the formation of the new body. But the old habits reasserted themselves. In the protocol creating the World Court there was what was called the "optional clause." Under this clause the nations which accepted it bound themselves to submit to arbitration all legal disputes. On August 14, 1946, the United States accepted this clause. The Senate then proceeded to reserve

all disputes . . . which are essentially within the domestic jurisdiction of the United States as determined by the United States of America, or disputes arising under a multilateral treaty unless all parties to the treaty affected by the decision are also parties to the case before the Court, or the United States of America specifically agrees to such jurisdiction.

I agree with one of our most distinguished students of international relations, Professor Hans Morgenthau, when he says that "it is hard to visualize an international dispute which might not be interpreted as to be covered" by these reservations. It is true that there has recently arisen a movement to withdraw these limitations on the Court's jurisdiction so far as the United States is concerned and that this movement has powerful support in the American Bar Association. But nothing in the past history of the arbitration movement entitles us to hope that this agitation will be successful.

Let us turn, then, from arbitration to another legal approach, that is, the drafting of agreements intended to restrain states from going to war.

The United States has, from time to time, attempted to limit the area of possible conflict by promoting agreements which reduce the possibility of war. Secretary of State Bryan negotiated a series of treaties popularly known as the "cooling-off treaties." These treaties provided that if a given dispute did not yield to the ordinary processes of diplomacy and could not be submitted to arbitration, the parties would submit the question to an investigatory commission and would agree not to go to war pending the investigation. These treaties met with little opposition in the Senate of the United States. It was an unusually hot summer in Washington. This may have affected the result.

This attempt to set legal limits to the invoking of war had, however, some conspicuous defects. In the first place, it hardly dealt effectively with what we shall have to describe as a continuing injury. Let me illustrate what I mean. Suppose that we had had, as we did not, one of these treaties with Germany at a time when the Reich had instituted submarine war. We could not be expected to permit the continued sinking of American vessels or the loss of American lives, while the commission was considering the matter. Or suppose a dispute arose over territory. It would be extremely trying to the patience of one of the disputants if the other party to the dispute continued to strengthen its position in the region in question while the controversy was under investigation.

In the second place, the Bryan proposal could hardly reach deep-seated conflicts of national interest. It could, in theory at least, be of some use in dealing with an international incident that had created a state of tension. If fact-finding were all that was involved, there might be a case for investigation. But in the most serious international controversies the desire for compromise may not even exist. The contest becomes a contest of will and power, rather than an appeal to reason. In such cases the issue has become sharpened to the point where national pride makes retreat difficult. Delay may leave the dispute unresolved—or even exacerbated.

There is an analogy to the Bryan treaties in the Covenant of the League of Nations, and since an American President (and a great one) had so much to do with the drafting of that instrument, we should consider it here. By the terms of the document, the members of the League agreed, in the event that a question should not

be susceptible of settlement by negotiation or by arbitration, that the Council of the League should consider the question. The Council was to make its report
within six months; in the elaboration of its report the
disputants were to have no negative; and it was further
stipulated that none of the parties to the dispute would
go to war until three months after the award. If the
report were unanimous, the contracting powers agreed
not to go to war with any disputant which accepted the
decision; if it were not unanimous they reserved "to
themselves the right to take such action as they shall
consider necessary for the maintenance of right and
justice." It would be pleasant to state that these provisions were faithfully observed; but the facts are otherwise. They proved ineffective in preventing the Japanese occupation of Manchuria in 1931, in the case of
the Italian attack on Ethiopia in 1935, and in the case
of the Russian attack on Finland in 1939, to mention
the most important cases. Though they called only for
a delay, and did not touch the right to go to war in any
absolute sense, they were none the less more than could
be exacted from the members of the international community in the thirties.

A much more ambitious effort to deal with the problem of war is to be found in the negotiation of the Kellogg-Briand pact of 1928, sometimes known as the Pact

[31]

of Paris. The history of this agreement is sufficiently instructive for us to consider it in some detail.

Here was a truly popular movement to deal with the evil of war. For those who believe (mistakenly, as I think) that the diplomats have a vested interest in controversy, and that the people, if they could be consulted, would find an answer to the problem of international conflict, it ought to be particularly instructive. For in this instance the policy that was adopted was forced upon a reluctant administration and represented a substantial body of public sentiment. That it failed to deal with the problem effectively will be evident as we proceed.

The movement for the outlawry of war, as it was called, stems from the establishment in December, 1921, of the American Committee for the Outlawry of War. The leader of this Committee was a Chicago businessman, Salmon O. Levinson. To Levinson the problem was simple. The answer to the age-old problem of international conflict was to make war illegal. Working with enormous energy, he rallied to his cause such people as John Dewey, Raymond Robins, John Haynes Holmes (the minister of New York's Community Church), Charles Clayton Morison, the editor of the *Christian Century,* and, somewhat hesitantly, Senator Borah of Idaho, one of the most influential figures in the fight against the League of Nations. For a time the cause made slow headway. But in 1927, the plan which he sponsored received great impetus with a proposal made by Briand, the French Foreign Minister. This proposal called for an agreement between France and the United States to renounce war in their relations with one another. The proposal, it will be observed, was for a limited agreement, applying to only two nations. It owed a good deal to the activities of one of the most pertinacious friends of international peace, Professor James T. Shotwell of Columbia University. Shotwell and his chief, President Nicholas Murray Butler of Columbia, did all that they could to publicize it and to bring pressure to bear upon the administration to accept the suggestion of the French Foreign Minister.

The administration received the Briand overture with a notable lack of enthusiasm. But substantial pressure developed in favor of some kind of positive action, and in the summer of 1927 the question was under discussion in the State Department, then under the direction of Frank B. Kellogg. The Secretary consulted J. Theodore Marriner, chief of the Division of Western European affairs, and received from him a memorandum suggesting that there could be little value in a two-power agreement and that if any further action was to be taken, "it should be in the form of an universal understanding not to resort to war, to which the United States would be most happy to become a party." For a long time thereafter the idea of outlawry simmered, while the inexhaustible Levinson and his friends continued their propaganda and built up a more and more formidable body of opinion in favor of their great idea.

New impetus was given to the grand design by a resolution of the League Assembly at the end of 1927 in which it was declared that "all wars of aggression are, and shall always be, prohibited." By November Senator Borah, who from his office in the Capitol wielded an enormous influence in foreign affairs, had come out in favor of a more generalized agreement similar to that which Briand had proposed. By December Kellogg, who stood in mortal fear of Borah, was galvanized into action. In answer to the French proposal of months before, he proposed to the French government that "the two Governments might make a more signal contribution to world peace by joining in an effort to obtain the adherence of all the principal powers of the world in a declaration renouncing war as an instrument of national policy." And with this declaration began a long negotiation that culminated in the so-called Kellogg-Briand pact of August 28, 1928.

The language of the Kellogg-Briand pact is simple in the extreme. By Article I the High Contracting Parties "solemnly declare in the name of their respective governments that they condemn recourse to war for the solution of international controversies, and renounce it as an instrument of national policy in their relations with one another." Article II states that "the High Contracting Parties agree that the settlement or solution of all disputes or conflicts of whatever nature or of whatever origin they may be, which may arise among them, shall never be sought except by pacific means."

The language of this important engagement has a certain charm. But in the discussions which preceded the signing of the pact there were, for the more sophisticated, clear warnings that the problem might not be as simple as it looked. In a remarkable speech of April 18, 1928, for example, Secretary Kellogg indicated that nothing in the proposed treaty subtracted in any way from the legitimate right of self-defense. But what was self-defense? Clearly any nation might claim, in any specific instance, that its resort to hostilities was in response to threatened danger. Self-defense had been from time immemorial one of the diplomatic formulas used to justify war. It seemed certain to many persons that it might so be used again.

The situation was further confused by interpretations of the pact by other governments. The British, for example, in signifying their readiness to adhere to the pact declared that "there are certain regions of the world the welfare and integrity of which constitute a special and vital interest to our peace and safety." They stated that:

His Majesty's Government have been at pains to make it clear in the past that interference with these regions cannot be suffered. Their protection against attack is to the British Empire a measure of self-defense. It must be clearly understood that His Majesty's Government in Great Britain accept the new treaty upon the distinct understanding that it does not prejudice their freedom of action in this respect.

Here was a large qualification indeed! Nor was it the only one. The French government made it clear that it remained bound by its alliances with other nations, and by the duty to act, possibly by force, in fulfilling the obligations of the Covenant of the League. The Japanese accepted the pact with the interpretation that it contained nothing that "would refuse to individual states the right of defense."

Nor was the position of the United States entirely unambiguous. Secretary Kellogg declared that every nation "is free at all times, and regardless of treaty provisions, to defend its territory against attack and invasion, and it alone is competent to decide whether circumstances require war in self-defense." The Senate also put in its word. It did not adopt formal reservations to the treaty, but when the pact was submitted to the Senate, the Senate Committee on Foreign Relations accompanied it with a gloss which declared among other things that "The United States regards the Monroe Doctrine as part of its national security and defense. Under the right of defense allowed by the treaty must necessarily be included the right to maintain the Monroe Doctrine which is a part of our national defense." Since the Doctrine had never been rigidly defined, this was an assertion of very considerable latitude in construing the pact.

Speaking generally, it is safe to say that the Kellogg pact was in no other country than the United States regarded as a solution of the problem of war. In the Senate it was ratified with enthusiasm, but Senator Reed of Missouri had the temerity to describe it as "an international kiss," and Senator Glass expressed doubts as to its efficacy.

I intend to vote for the peace pact [announced the Senator], but I am not willing that anybody in Virginia shall think that I am simple enough to suppose that it is worth a postage stamp in the direction of accomplishing permanent peace. I think we are about to renounce something as a national policy which no nation on earth for 150 years has ever proclaimed as a national policy. . . . But I am going to be simple enough, along with the balance of you, to vote for the ratification of this worthless, but perfectly harmless peace treaty.

Senator Glass's comment on the Kellogg-Briand pact was, I regret to say, for the most part vindicated by events. It could be argued, perhaps, that by branding war as illegal, it prepared the way for the acceptance by the United States of some responsibility to take action against an aggressor nation; certainly this is what some of the proponents of the pact hoped for. But when practical issues arose involving the breach of the peace, it proved of little value. It played no part whatever in the diplomatic discussions which preceded the outbreak of the Second World War.

The very year after it was signed, hostilities broke out between the Soviet Union and the Chinese government. Secretary Stimson called the attention of the disputants to their obligations under the treaty of Paris and although at the outset he received a soft answer, the quarrel went on. When, a little later, he again appealed to the two parties, and persuaded Great Britain, France, and Italy to follow his lead, he got nowhere. The Chinese government denied it had broken the pact; the Russian government, in a sharply worded note, informed the government of the United States that the matter was none of its business. "The govern-

ment of the Soviet Union states further that the Paris
Pact does not give to any single state or group of states
the function of protector of this pact. The Soviet government, at any rate, never expressed consent that any
States themselves or by mutual consent should take
upon themselves such a right."

Similarly, the Kellogg pact proved to be a broken
reed when in 1931 a dispute arose between the Japanese
and the Chinese over Manchuria. This controversy I
shall examine in more detail in my second chapter. Suf-
fice it to say here that when the Japanese overran all
Manchuria, in which up to 1931 they had strictly limited rights, invocations of the Kellogg pact did not ar-
rest this movement, nor prevent the ultimate establishment of a puppet regime there directly subservient to
Japan.

In the controversies of the thirties the Paris pact
played a very subordinate role. It did not prevent international wars from breaking out on an increasing scale,
the Italian war with Ethiopia in 1935, the Sino-Japa-
nese war in 1937, the Second World War in 1939. Nor,
so far as my knowledge extends, did the United States
after 1931 directly involve it in correspondence with
any other government.

We must not, however, in stressing the weakness of
the Kellogg pact, go too far in our criticism. The treaty

undoubtedly expressed the strong moral aversion of the peoples of the world to war; no government dared to do less than give it lip service. In expressing this aversion, if it did not prevent war, it stamped it with an immoral character; and it forms an important step in the breaking down of the old concepts of neutrality, and in the development of the view that a nation which willfully breaks the peace must not expect to be dealt with on the same terms as a nation which is clearly and obviously the victim of aggression. Putting the matter in another way, the Paris pact prepared the way for new norms of conduct in international relations.

But it is significant that it took some time for these new norms to become at all acceptable, so far as the United States was concerned. On the contrary, in the 1930's the American government embarked upon a course of policy which, instead of distinguishing between the aggressor and its victim, and applying different standards of conduct to the one and the other, was almost fanatically devoted to the maintenance and extension of the principle of neutrality, on the ground that this was the way to keep out of war. The story is one that needs telling.

In the 1930's there took place a period of disillusionment with regard to the entry of the United States into the First World War. The feeling grew that the treaty of Versailles was an unsatisfactory settlement of the conflict, that the war, far from producing a more peaceful era, had raised up a crop of new disputes, that the true interest of the American people lay, as it had always lain, in abstention from participation in the politics of Europe, and that the nation must be safeguarded against making the same mistakes that it had committed in 1914–17, which had finally led to its participation in the war. This point of view was given much currency by the activities of the so-called Nye committee, which, appointed in 1934 to examine the question of the role of the munition-makers in the promotion of war, proceeded to go far beyond its mandate, and to draw very wide conclusions indeed as to what was necessary for the preservation of peace. The administration was by no means wholly of the same mind as the majority in Congress; it was anxious, indeed, in the drafting of new legislation, to discriminate or to differentiate between an aggressor nation and its victim; but it was not able to impose its view on Congress.

What was the result? Congress sought to prevent war by legislating against the supposed errors of twenty years before. Because, as it was alleged, the munitions manufacturers had had a part in influencing the events of the second decade, there was to be a strict embargo on weapons of war. Because, as it was alleged, the influence of the great bankers had been powerfully exerted in favor of our entrance into the conflict, and loans on a substantial scale had been made to the Allied governments, there was to be a strict prohibition on loans to belligerent governments. Because insistence by the American government on the right of Americans to travel on belligerent merchant ships had led to a controversy with Germany, and finally to war, the President was first empowered, and later required, to forbid such travel. Because, as it was alleged, trade with the Allied powers conditioned the United States in favor of those powers, trade with future belligerents was to be curtailed. The legislation which imposed these various restraints on governmental action was passed by immense majorities in both houses of Congress, and signed by the President.

It is hardly necessary to recall the melancholy history of this legislation. When war broke out in Europe, it was speedily realized by important elements in America, and surely by the President of the United States, that the safety of the nation lay in the defeat of the German dictator who had so wantonly provoked war. What happened? First, the embargo was repealed. Second, the lend-lease enactment of the winter of 1941 made mincemeat of the trade provisions of the previous legislation, and of the prohibition of loans to belligerents. Third, the United States proceeded to take an increasingly active part against the German submarine warfare on the seas, and was indeed in a state of informal warfare with Germany two months before the Japanese attack on Pearl Harbor. The notion that the way to deal with the problem of peace was to legislate neutrality received a body blow, from which it has never recovered.

There is something more to be said. It cannot be maintained—because we do not know—that if the United States had made it clear that it would line up with the Western powers against German aggression, the aggression would not have occurred. Certainly the policies of France and Great Britain were tragically weak and ineffectual in the years from 1933 to 1939. But we *can* say that American neutrality legislation of the thirties amounted to putting the German dictator on notice—for the time being—that he had nothing to fear from the United States, and that its possible effect was to embolden him to upset the peace of the world.

What, then, are the general conclusions to be drawn from our discussion thus far? First of all, it may be stated that nothing in the experience of the last half century suggests that the United States, any more than any other nation, is ready to submit its disputes to arbitration or to judicial settlement. The plain fact of the matter is that the really significant divergences between nations involve questions for which the corpus of international law is not adequate. They are not disputes in the purely legal sense of the term. They are questions which transcend purely legal considerations. Such questions, writes Professor Brierly, one of the most acute students of international law, are not usually settled by "an authoritarian act."

The cause of the prevention of war has very little to gain from improved international machinery for "settlement" if by that word we mean the process by which the decision of a tribunal of some sort is imposed upon the parties interested. Tribunals can settle mere "disputes" but they cannot settle the complicated questions out of which wars arise. This is not to say that these situations cannot be controlled, but only that we underrate the difficulty and mistake the nature of the task of controlling them if we allow ourselves to think of it in terms that suggest the authority either of a tribunal or of a majority.

The considerations which I have just brought to your attention are more compelling than they were a half century ago. For the plain fact of the matter is that the Soviet Union, the Chinese Peoples' Republic, and other Communist governments do not proceed on the basis that the problems of our international life are to be settled by legal means. The chance that they would agree to the extension of the area of international law, except where it most served their interests, is very small indeed.

Nor, on the basis of the past, does there seem much chance that the formal machinery of conciliation, such as was suggested by the Bryan treaties, has any very extended possibilities in the prevailing state of the world. What we must expect in dealing with the Communist states is that important issues will be dealt with, if dealt with at all, not by specially devised machinery, but by the process of long, protracted, and difficult negotiation. Such negotiation may, on occasion, produce results, as was the case, for example, with the Soviet withdrawal from Austria. But the process here is the time-tested process of give-and-take, not based upon legal principles but upon the coincidence of national interests, as they are conceived by the parties at the time.

Nor are pledges not to go to war to be depended upon to produce significant results. The Kellogg-Briand pact serves as an example of this truth.

Were I to terminate at this point, it is certain that you would derive very little comfort from it—and very little guidance. But what I have been trying to do is to sweep away illusion. We cannot deal effectively with any problem if we proceed on false premises. We may

cheerfully admit that international law is indispensable
to the intercourse of states. We may cheerfully admit
that its principles are observed (though partly because
its reach is so modest). We may cheerfully admit that
it provides a means for settling some controversies.
We may applaud any effort to extend the area in which
it operates. But with regard to the central problem of
war prevention, we must say quite frankly that it is a
palliative. It does not go to the heart of the problem.
Nor, as I see it, is it likely to do so in any foreseeable
period. We shall have to look further if we wish to ap-
praise the success of the American people in dealing
with the problem of international peace. We shall have
to examine the principle of collective security.

# ⁓ 2 ⁓
# Peace through Collective Security

IN THE OPTIMISTIC CLIMATE OF THE END of the nineteenth century it is not strange that men thought that peace could be secured through law. So deep-seated was this feeling that it survived the First World War, expressed itself in a powerful way in the Kellogg-Briand pact, and has still its advocates at the present day. But side by side with this conviction there grew up another, which was destined to have a wide influence on international relations and which has shown immense vitality. This was the idea of "collective security," the idea that the way to peace was through an organization of nations which should band together to take action against an aggressor. The analogy here to civil society is not perfect but it is suggestive. The advocates of this idea pointed out that the tranquillity of a community rested upon the creation of a police force which could take action against wrongdoers; why not then create in some fashion an international police force which would put down violence in the international sphere?

It is interesting that one of the first expressions of this idea came from Theodore Roosevelt. Speaking at Christiania, Norway, at the time of his receipt of the Nobel Peace Prize, Roosevelt declared that it would be a master stroke if the great powers honestly bent on peace "would form a League of Peace, not only to keep peace among themselves but to prevent, by force if necessary, its being broken by others." While this statement was widely applauded at the time, it does not appear to have had any substantial influence. It needed the outbreak of World War to stimulate widespread discussion of the idea.

In the winter of 1915, at the instance of Hamilton Holt, editor of the *Independent,* a group of men met to draw up a program. This program called for the settlement of all disputes by amicable means and for the use of force, if necessary, against a nation which resorted to war. At a later meeting this program was accepted by such distinguished men as William Howard Taft and Abbott Lawrence Lowell, President of Harvard. An organization, the League to Enforce Peace, was set up to agitate for the acceptance of a program which explicitly declared in favor of coercive action against a nation which refused to arbitrate its disputes or to submit them to some process of conciliation. Ex-President Taft became the President of the new body, President Lowell wrote an article supporting its purposes in the *Atlantic Monthly* in September, 1915, and the United States Chamber of Commerce was persuaded to endorse the program, at least in part. In May of 1916 a great meeting was held in Washington and President Wilson was invited to address it. There, in the presence of a distinguished assemblage, in language that was still somewhat cautious but which pointed directly toward the endorsement of the idea, Wilson declared that the United States would be ready to become a "partner in any feasible association of nations." When he was renominated at St. Louis less than two months later, the Democratic platform contained a similar pronouncement.

The interest of the President in the League idea was much strengthened by the drift toward American participation in the war against Germany. In his great speech of January 22, 1917, before the die had been cast, he endorsed the League idea with more precision than ever before and in the war address of the 2nd of April he declared that the object of the war was to "set up among the really free and self-governed peoples of the world such a concert of purpose and action as will henceforth insure the observance of the principles of peace and justice." What lesser object than this could justify the sacrifices to which America had now been called?

We need not examine in detail the further evolution of Wilson's thought during the war period except for one highly important point. In the President's mind there loomed large the idea of a territorial guarantee. This idea was to be found in some of his earlier correspondence and some of his private utterances. But it is stated with great explicitness in the speech of the Fourteen Points, delivered on January 6, 1918. Laying down terms for ending of war, Wilson declared that "a general association of nations must be formed under specific covenants for the purpose of affording mutual guarantees of political independence and territorial integrity to great and small nations alike." When it came to the negotiation of the armistice in the fall of 1918, a pledge to this end was inserted in the armistice agreement itself. And with the ending of the war Wilson went abroad to fight for what, beyond all question, he considered as the greatest objective to which he had ever dedicated himself.

We need not follow in minute detail the long discussions which took place at Paris and which resulted in the Covenant of the League of Nations. The document which was finally drafted by a commission presided over by the President bore more than one mark of Wilson's special influence. Its general principles were these. The League of Nations, as conceived in the Covenant, was open to the nations which had signed the treaty of Versailles and to all others by a two-thirds vote of the Assembly, provided that they accepted the obligations of the Covenant itself. The governing bodies of the League were the Council, in which the great powers would have five out of eleven seats, and the Assembly, in which all states would be represented. The members of the League agreed to "respect and preserve as against external aggression the existing political independence and territorial integrity of the members of the League." They agreed to submit their disputes to either arbitration or conciliation, to be bound by an arbitral award, and not to go to war against the other party to a dispute if the process of conciliation resulted in a unanimous judgment. They agreed that if any member of the League resorted to war in violation of its engagements it should *ipso facto* be deemed to have committed an act of war against all members of the League, and that they would undertake immediately to subject it to "the severance of all trade or financial relations, the prohibition of all intercourse between their nationals and the nationals of the Covenant-breaking state, and the prevention of all financial, commercial or personal intercourse between the nationals of the Covenant-breaking state and the nationals of any other state, whether a member of the League or not." To this article there was added a statement that "It shall be the duty of the Council in such case to recommend to the several Governments concerned what effective military, naval or air force the members of the League shall severally contribute to the armed forces to be used to protect the Covenants of the League."

Such, in highly compressed form, are the principal provisions of the Covenant as far as the principle of collective security is concerned. They deserve comment.

Article X of the Covenant guaranteeing the territorial integrity of the members of the League was to be the center of attack on the part of the League's foes in the United States. It was sometimes said that it froze the *status quo* and consecrated injustice, and this argument was particularly effective since the territorial terms of the treaty of Versailles soon came under severe criticism. It was said that the commitment was altogether too far-reaching, involving the American government in intervention all over the world. There was an answer to both these contentions. To the first it might with reason be said that all that Article X did was to prevent change in the *status quo by violence*. It did not prevent *adjustment* of frontiers, merely their forcible alteration. Using the analogy of civil society, what was wrong with that? We do not permit an aggrieved person to take the law into his own hands, whatever the character of the grievance. As to the second point, the wide extent of the commitment, was it not reasonable to suppose that in actual practice the nations with the most direct interest in a given territorial problem would be the ones to assume the principal burden of punishing the aggressor? Was this not the only logical course, in fact?

On abstract grounds, then, we need not take the view of the League critics with regard to Article X. But what we must say is this. It dramatized the fact that under the Covenant the United States would have a much wider responsibility for world order than it ever had had before. It is not strange, perhaps, that the American people were not prepared to undertake so heavy a

[55]

burden, taking into consideration their isolationist past.

The machinery to be directed against an aggressor under the Covenant betrays a deeper weakness. The major emphasis is economic. There seems to be a distinct drawing back from the use of physical force. The language in this latter case is vague. There is every reason to believe that Wilson placed more faith than he should have in the value of economic pressure. We shall have more to say of this later.

Finally, in the prescriptions for membership, there lurks a fundamental problem. The language of the Covenant called for the admission of "self-governing nations." Did this mean democratic nations? The question is not an idle one. In his great war address, Wilson had declared that a secure league of peace could only be a league of democratic nations. Otherwise, "intrigue would eat its vitals away." Did some such conception lie in that little word "self-governing"? If so, the subsequent history of the League ran counter to Wilson's thought. Some of the nations admitted to membership forthwith could only by a generous use of words be described as self-governing. I dwell upon this question because it suggests one of the great difficulties with the idea of collective security, that is, the wide difference of outlook that exists between a democratic and a totalitarian state. Can both cooperate in the enforcement of world peace? Or are the initial assumptions too great to be bridged?

The question is more timely today than it seemed then. Much of the world seemed to League enthusiasts ready in 1919 to accept the Wilsonian principles. If the League fell short of universality, might it not all the same accomplish great good? So we argued forty years ago. So we hoped.

I shall not enter in detail into the League struggle in the United States. Yet here, as in our discussion of the rule of law, we might pause to reflect upon the fact that Americans, for all their idealism, were not ready to make the sacrifices demanded of them. Article X dramatized the difficulty. It was a sound tactical instinct that led the Republican opposition to fix its attention on this article. It seemed to involve a great departure from the past and to suggest great sacrifices. It was useless, and it seems now a bit of semantics, for Wilson to explain that the obligation of the article was moral, not legal. Why accept a moral obligation, if one intended to skate away from it on the ground that there was no legal duty to act? The question was a pertinent one.

The friends of the League had their answer, perhaps a good one. (I certainly thought it a good one at the time.) Why not make the magnanimous gesture of assuming a wide responsibility for the peace of the world? Might it not be that if we made the gesture others would follow?

We shall never know. Yet the League idea showed immense vitality, even after the Covenant itself had been rejected by the people of the United States. In 1924 the League nations drew up a document known as the Geneva Protocol. It was approved unanimously. It provided for the extension of the compulsory jurisdiction of the Court of International Justice, for the settlement, either by the Council of the League or by compulsory arbitration, of all disputes which did not fall within the jurisdiction of the Court. At the same time it made it possible to define an aggressor with more precision than the Covenant had done and bound the signatories to participate loyally and effectively in the application of sanctions, but with the proviso that aid should be given by each state "in the degree to which its geographical position and particular situation as regards armament allows." It has always been for me a melancholy chapter in our diplomatic history that when the British ambassador at Washington sought from Secretary of State Hughes his opinion of the protocol, Hughes declared that it might lead to a concert of action against the United States and interfere with American trade. Hughes's position was sustained by

President Coolidge. Let us remember these facts, and not forget that we sometimes appear to others to be among the unco guid.

It is possible, though not probable, that a different attitude on the part of the United States in the 1920's would have prevented the painful events of two decades later. But we have to deal with history as it is, and I must now narrate the story of the collective security idea with strict reference to the facts and to the conclusions to which those facts point.

The first serious test of the principle of collective security came in 1931. In that year the Japanese, who possessed restricted rights in the Chinese province of Manchuria, proceeded to overrun and take possession of the whole area. We have already seen that the United States invoked the Briand-Kellogg pact on this occasion without conspicuous success. What was the position of the League, to which the Chinese naturally appealed?

No one can read the account of the events of the next few months without observing how cautiously the Geneva organization handled the whole problem. That there had been aggression seemed incontestable and this impression was confirmed as time went on, and the Japanese, while the Council of the League debated, proceeded to extend their control more and more fully over Manchuria. Yet the first step of the League was not to invoke the punitive provisions of the Covenant but to act under Article 11, which called for a special meeting of the Council in the event of any threat to the peace. The Council met September 22, by a unanimous vote called upon the Chinese and Japanese governments to "refrain from any action which might aggravate the situation or prejudice the peaceful settlement of the problem," and authorized M. Lerroux, its President, "to endeavor, in consultation with the Chinese and Japanese governments, to find adequate means of enabling the two countries to withdraw their troops immediately, without the lives of their nationals and the safety of their property being endangered."

This appeal was without important effect; the Japanese responded with a statement that they would withdraw their troops when the safety of their nationals was assured, but at the same time they continued to advance; only two days after the Council resolution a passenger train on the Peking-Mukden rail line was bombed, and on October 8 the city of Chinchow, remote from the rail line, was attacked from the air in a raid of substantial proportions. In the meantime the Council had met again, had passed another pious resolution, and had determined to hold a third session on October 14. This session was postponed for a few days but on the 16th the Council did indeed convene and debated the Manchurian situation at length. This time its action went a little further than before; after the usual references to the will to peace on both sides, the Council called upon the Japanese government "to begin immediately and to proceed progressively with the withdrawal of its troops into the railway zone, so that the total withdrawal may be effected before the date fixed for the next meeting of the Council." This date was fixed as November 16.

Again the action of the League agency was defied. On the 21st of October, the Japanese authorities proceeded to send to Peiping the effects of the young Marshal Chang Hsueh-liang, the nominal governor of Manchuria, a gentle hint that his role was being liquidated; extended their military operations to points as distant as 300 miles from the railroad lines; and clashed with the Chinese at the Nonni bridge, far away from the original area of operations. Under Article 11 of the Covenant, the only article that had been invoked, they could claim that they had not defied the Council but the position in which the League found itself was none the less humiliating. At no time did any member of the Council, in any of the meetings which we have mentioned, discuss invoking the punitive provisions of Articles 15 and 16 and during the period we have mentioned, the British government recalled Lord Robert

Cecil, a militant friend of the League, and replaced him with Sir John Simon, who, then and later, can be fairly described as an apostle of appeasement.

It was necessary, then, to find a way to save the League's face, and in a new meeting of the Council, which began November 21, after a prolonged debate it was decided to appoint a commission to investigate the dispute and report back to the Council. In the meantime the Japanese continued to consolidate their position in Manchuria. Moreover, in January of 1932 fighting broke out in the neighborhood of Shanghai; in other words the Japanese extended their operations to the Chinese mainland.

What, during these events, was the position of the United States? Henry L. Stimson, the Secretary of State, had always been sympathetic to the idea of collective security and he strove to cooperate with Geneva. From the beginning of the Manchurian outbreak, he was in close touch with Sir Eric Drummond, the Secretary-General at Geneva; he paralleled his protests with those of the Council of the League, and on October 5 he sent a remarkable letter to Drummond.

The Covenant of the League [he wrote] provides permanent and already tested machinery for handling such issues as between state members of the League. . . . The Council has formulated conclusions and outlined a course of action to be followed by the disputants; and as the said disputants have made commitments to the Council, it is most desirable that the League in no way relax its vigilance and in no way fail to assert all the pressure and authority within its competence towards regulating the action of China and Japan in the premises. On its part the American government acting independently through its diplomatic representative will endeavor to re-inforce what the League does, and will make clear that it has a keen interest in the matter.

For the moment, Stimson went further. At his suggestion the Council of the League invited an American observer to sit in at its sessions. On October 16 the American consul at Geneva, Prentiss Gilbert, took his seat with the members of the Council and continued to attend its sessions up to the 24th.

But Stimson's action meant less than it seemed to mean at the time. He was later to explain that the phrase "exert all the pressure and authority within its competence," as applied to League action, meant no more than the exercise of moral pressure. He stated that Gilbert would participate in discussion only in a limited way, when engagements such as the Kellogg-Briand pact were being considered. He would not commit the United States to the support of any form of punitive action. And, as the anti-League voices in America made themselves heard, he shifted his position once again and instructed Charles Gates Dawes to go to Paris as an observer but not to take any direct part in the deliberations of the Council.

The fact is that the American administration was not ready to do anything really effective. President Hoover was strongly opposed to the application of any sanctions against Japan. Stimson may, for a brief time, have hoped that economic pressure would be used to bring the Tokyo government to heel. But he never intimated that the United States would support such action; the most that he was willing to do was to tell Dawes in private, and under an injunction not to divulge his views, that if the League applied an embargo against Japan, the American government would probably put no obstacle in the way of such action.

Indeed, he went off on a tangent of his own. In January of 1932 he addressed a letter to Senator Borah, Chairman of the Foreign Relations Committee of the Senate, in which he declared that the United States would not recognize "any situation, treaty, or agreement entered into in violation of the rights of the United States in the Far East." In default of any better course, the Assembly of the League adopted in March of 1932 a resolution which, in broader terms, stated the non-recognition doctrine as it had been laid down by the Secretary of State. Such action was ineffective.

True, the Japanese withdrew from Shanghai, where they had met with rough going from the Chinese; but in Manchuria they pursued determinedly the course on which they had entered. They set up a puppet regime in that province and when the commission appointed by the League under the resolution of November 22 made its report, they declined to accept the findings or recommendations and after a heated and dramatic debate withdrew from the League itself.

The question naturally arises whether the United States might have taken a more determined stand. But the answer to the question is almost certainly no. Looking at the matter from the domestic political angle, it is doubtful that American public opinion of the time would have sustained any such position. To reiterate, the President, who would have had to give a lead in the matter, was vigorously opposed to such action. Even if we discount these considerations, it is clear that the great European powers had no stomach for punitive action against Japan. Neither the British nor the French, who were the powers with the largest interests in the Far East, ever suggested such a thing. The Secretary-General of the League, who was in close touch with the various governments, expressed himself in private as opposed to economic coercion, and the Chinese themselves never sought to invoke those articles of the Covenant which would have opened the way to the application of sanctions. All in all, the League proved ineffective in the hour of challenge.

It was possible to argue that this first decisive defiance of the Geneva organization occurred under very unfavorable circumstances. From the legal side, it could be contended that there had been no declaration of war, in the literal sense, and that the punitive provisions of the Covenant did not apply; it could be contended that China's action in Manchuria had long been provocative; that her misrule in that province afforded an excuse for Japan; and that, in any case, to quote a distinguished critic, "It was obviously impossible . . . to apply the sanctions of the Covenant in the case of an obscure and complicated dispute between two Oriental peoples." It could also be pointed out that the test came at a time when the Great Depression had engulfed a large part of the world, when the political situation in the United States, France, and Great Britain, was distressful, and when, therefore, governments were disposed not to take any unnecessary risks, or face any avoidable perils.

But the considerations which we have mentioned apply with much diminished force to the next challenge which was made to the League and in which the attempt to exert its authority again resulted in a fiasco.

This was the Italian invasion of Ethiopia in the fall of 1935.

The Italian dictator, Mussolini, whatever he may have done to produce stability in his own country, had an itch for conquest which in the long run was to ruin him. His first manifestation of this spirit came as early as 1923, when he seized the island of Corfu, on the basis of certain flimsy claims against the Greek government. On that occasion he was forced to back down and the League played a part in his capitulation; no doubt the bitter memory of this episode influenced his determination to defy the Geneva organization at some later time. The Italians had attempted to get possession of Ethiopia as early as 1895, but they had sustained there a crushing military defeat. To avenge this defeat may also have been a motive with the dictator. At any rate, in 1935 he picked a quarrel with the government at Addis Ababa. On October 6, 1935, Italian airplanes bombarded Ethiopian territory and not much later Italian troops crossed the frontier. Here was a direct challenge to the Geneva organization.

The League met the challenge with at least somewhat more resolution than it had shown in 1931. On October 7 the Council approved a report declaring that Italy had resorted to war in violation of the Covenant. It thus opened the way to the application of sanctions, and November 18 was set as the day on which these sanctions would be applied if Italy did not respect her obligations. Since the Rome government remained defiant, the Council went further. It declared an arms embargo against Italy, an embargo on all Italian exports, an embargo on credit, and an embargo on the export to Italy of certain raw materials. But what it did *not* do was to apply an embargo on the export of oil, the most essential of all raw materials for the prosecution of the war. This failure, of course, expressed the irresolution of the governments concerned, and their reluctance to push matters to an extreme. The French and the British were watching with apprehension the growth of the power of Adolf Hitler in Germany; and they could not make up their minds to take action which might throw the Italian government into the arms of the German Fuehrer. Moreover, Mussolini threatened war if oil were embargoed, and for war neither France nor Great Britain were prepared.

What London and Paris did, however, was to compound impotence with perfidy. The foreign ministers of the two countries proceeded to work out a deal by which, in large measure, Italian demands would be satisfied. An explosion of indignation followed, especially in Great Britain; Sir Samuel Hoare, the author of the deal and the Foreign Secretary, was obliged to resign. The episode was a striking illustration of weakness and in the course of the year 1936 the Italians, in defiance of League action, overran all Ethiopia and established their rule there. There was to come a day when, in a confession of defeat, the sanctions were withdrawn and the Ethiopian question brought to an inglorious end. The principal effect of this whole episode was to throw Mussolini into the arms of Hitler, and to permit the German dictator to occupy the Rhineland, which had been demilitarized under the treaty of Versailles and which ought to have remained so. In diplomacy, even more than in life in general, it is fatal to start something that you cannot finish, and this was precisely what the League had done in the dispute just considered.

What was the attitude of the United States in this second challenge to the Geneva organization? Before answering this question it is necessary to say that, in the face of European irresolution, it is quite unfair to place any major responsibility on the American government; yet the American attitude is interesting, none the less. The Roosevelt administration never openly expressed sympathy with the League; it never encouraged directly the application of sanctions; indeed, Secretary Hull explicitly refused to commit himself on this matter. By indirection the United States sought to assist the

League cause. Under existing laws, it was possible for the President to declare an arms embargo, if it were applied to both belligerents; and this Roosevelt did, of course to the detriment of the Italian cause. It was possible, also, to urge a moral embargo on shipments to Italy, and this step was taken, not altogether effectually, as the event proved. It was possible to discourage oil shipments to Italy. While the dispute was going on, the administration played with the idea of limiting oil exports by law to the amounts used in time of peace. But none of these measures was effective and all of them fell far short of any public endorsement of the attitude of the League, or of any prodding of the French and British governments to show firmness in dealing with the government at Rome. Once again the American government had shown timidity in dealing with the League and once again it had failed to exert any effective influence on the side of collective security.

The Ethiopian fiasco marks, indeed, the collapse of the League as an effective force for peace. It is not necessary to follow the melancholy story of the years 1936–39, of Hitler's increasing violence and increasing success and of the outbreak of the Second World War in 1939. When the Russians ruthlessly invaded Finland in the fall of 1939, the League read them out of the world organization; but the organization itself was but a shell and it did not survive the war.

Yet the idea of collective security survived and in 1945 the nations of the world met at San Francisco to draft a new instrument which would embody the principles of the Covenant and offer to the war-weary peoples of the world a new hope of peace. The result, as we know, was the Charter of the United Nations.

In its structure, the United Nations organization bears certain resemblances to the League. There is a Council, composed of five permanent members: China, France, the U.S.S.R., Great Britain, and the United States; and six elective members. There is an Assembly in which all "peace-loving" states may be represented. But the emphasis on collective security is somewhat different. "The Council," reads Article 24 of the Charter, "is charged with primary responsibility for the maintenance of peace," and the members of the new organization agree that "in carrying out its duties under this responsibility the Security Council acts on their behalf." Here was a grant of wide powers. But just because the grant was a wide one, it was necessary, in order to ensure acceptance of the Charter by the great powers, to provide that all decisions of the Council must be taken by the concurring votes of the five permanent members. Here is the origin of what has come to be called the veto.

The permanent veto was no less acceptable to the United States in 1945 than it was to the Soviet Union; indeed, it must always remain doubtful whether the Charter could have been ratified without it. But it has resulted, over a period of years, in greatly restricting the role of the Security Council itself. The powers of the Council to act for the international community have become illusory so far as positive and united action to prevent aggression is concerned. "The result of insisting that only a body that had power to make binding decisions could act effectively," says Professor Brierly, with some exaggeration but with much truth, "has been to give us a body that can neither decide nor act."

The framers of the Charter not only intended to give to the Security Council a central role; they also thought that they were avoiding the errors of the Covenant in laying the emphasis on physical coercion of an aggressor rather than on economic sanctions. In this they were essentially right. There is no greater fallacy than the fallacy that economic coercion can be an effective and dependable means of bringing an international wrong-doer to terms. If we look back on our own history, we shall find an illustration of this fact. For one thing, economic pressure is slow in its effects. Henry Adams raised this point years ago, and with brilliance, in his monumental study of the administrations of Jefferson and Madison. "The law of physics could be applied to politics," he wrote. "Force could be converted only into its equivalent force. If the embargo—an exertion of force—were to do the work of war, it must extend over a longer time an equivalent energy." Over this longer time, economic sanctions, moreover, invite evasion; they do not unify national opinion to the degree that war does; and they may even lead to violence. It seems likely that the American severance of economic relations with Japan in 1941 brought Pearl Harbor nearer, rather than contributing to the prolongation of peace.

However this may be, the Charter contemplated the creation of a genuine international force, at the disposal of the Security Council. "The members of the United Nations," reads Article 43, "in order to contribute to international peace and security, undertake to make available to the Security Council, on its call, and in accordance with a special agreement or agreements, armed forces, assistance and facilities, including rights of passage, necessary for the purpose of maintaining international peace and security." "In order to enable the United Nations to take urgent military measures," reads Article 45, "members shall hold immediately available national air-force contingents for combined international enforcement action." The Charter goes on to provide for the establishment of a Military Staff Committee to advise and assist the Security Council.

It is scarcely necessary to say that this ambitious scheme for the enforcement of peace through an international body clothed with large authority has not worked out in practice. Nor does there seem any immediate prospect that the situation will change. But it is worth noting that a modest beginning has been made in the creation of an international force. After the Anglo-French-Israeli imbroglio over the Suez canal in 1956, a United Nations military contingent was sent to the Gaza strip and the Gulf of Aqaba to maintain peaceful conditions there. It still remains, and it has performed a useful service.* But this is a far cry from the scheme laid down in the Charter.

There is of course, one key example of the application of the collective security principle in the events that occurred in Korea in 1950. In June of that year the North Koreans invaded the state of South Korea, which had at that time been recognized as a duly organized government by the United Nations itself.

---

* In the Congo, too, a United Nations force has performed a positive service, though under great difficulties.

President Truman immediately asked for a meeting of the Security Council. Such a meeting was held and a resolution, sponsored by the United States, was adopted which denounced the North Korean action as a breach of the peace and called upon the members of the United Nations to "render every assistance . . . in the execution of this resolution and to refrain from giving assistance to the North Korean authorities." On the 27th the Council went further. It passed a new resolution calling upon the members of the United Nations to "furnish such assistance to the Republic of Korea as may be necessary to repel the armed attack and to restore international peace and security." Acting under this resolution the United States first sent air and naval forces to the assistance of the hard-pressed Korean government and three days later the President ordered General MacArthur to land troops in Korea. On the 7th of July the Council designated General MacArthur as the commander of all U.N. forces in the peninsula.

What was the response of the other members of the United Nations to the appeal made to them? Of the more than fifty nations then members, only fifteen sent forces to participate in the war. Many of these were token forces only. The fighting in Korea was largely conducted by the United States and the South Koreans. Their troops constituted about 90 per cent of the total.

Their troops suffered 96 per cent of the casualties. The action of the United Nations in Korea, to put it bluntly, was wholly dependent upon the attitude of the United States. Without the resolute stand taken by President Truman, the Council would have been as impotent to deal with the situation as was the Council of the League in the case of Manchuria or of Ethiopia. Collective action was to a substantial extent a façade behind which the American forces operated.

But there is more to the matter than that. Any action whatsoever under the Charter would have been impossible had it not been for a happy accident. The Russians at this time were sulking because the Chinese Communists had not been recognized and admitted to the United Nations. Their representative was absent from the Council. Had he been present, under the terms of the Charter he could have used the veto to prevent the proposed action. He could conceivably have hamstrung the whole operation.

Moreover, in the long run the United Nations action in Korea fell short of complete success. In the first months of the fighting, after an initial retreat, it seemed as if the forces under MacArthur would bring off a substantial victory. The declared objective of these forces was to unify all Korea. The Council authorized a resolution which implicitly approved this aim. But in

[76]

November the Chinese Communists entered the war. What followed is well known. After months more of fighting, the United States, acting as the representative of the United Nations, negotiated the armistice, which left the boundary much as it had been before. Since that time, the terms of the armistice have been consistently flouted by the Chinese, though there has been no resumption of hostilities.

It was well recognized in Washington that the opportunity afforded by the Russian absence from the Council table would, in all probability, not occur again. Accordingly, Secretary Acheson promoted the passage of a resolution in the Assembly, by which, if the Security Council did not act, the Assembly, by a two-thirds vote, could apply the sanctions of the Covenant. We do not know whether or not this machinery could be successfully invoked. As the United Nations has admitted more and more members, and as the tendency of the new members seems frequently to be toward neutralism, it would be increasingly difficult to muster such a vote. But in any case, it seems clear from the experience in Korea that anything like effective action in the application of the principle of collective security must depend upon a few nations and that only a very little assistance is to be expected from many.

There is another point to be made. As is well

known, friction arose between General MacArthur and the Truman administration. General MacArthur wished to pursue the war vigorously against the Chinese, blockading their coast, bombing their supply dumps, employing, if possible, the Chinese Nationalists against them. President Truman and his military advisers, on the other hand, mindful of the necessity of cooperating with other powers, and of the situation in Europe where we had important allies, wished to pursue a different course. This demonstrates that the collective security doctrine imposes some limits on the freedom of action of the principal powers engaged in enforcing the principle. The strain need not be considered as intolerable but that it exists, and would always exist, is undeniable.

Let me make it clear that, in dealing with this matter, I am not condemning the action of the administration. The question of the wisdom of President Truman's action will be long debated by the historians. There is a strong case for the theory (a case which I personally would espouse) that if the United States had tolerated aggression in Korea, it would have opened up a Pandora's box of evils. One may well believe this, and yet see that in the last analysis it was the United States and not the United Nations which was responsible for meeting the challenge, and for the consequences—good or evil—that flowed from it.

Yet the principle of collective security conceals or contains a significant principle—the principle of association with other powers for the maintenance of peace. This principle the American people were long reluctant to recognize. During the greater part of their history they have been unwilling to combine their own force with the force of others in the interest of world stability. They did, indeed, ally themselves with France in the War of the American Revolution, and this alliance was a potent factor in the final victory. But not long thereafter, there grew up the dogma that the true interest of the United States lay in abstention from any political connection with any other power. The dogma, it may be admitted, had some relevance in the conditions of the nineteenth century. But it has been proven false in the conditions of the twentieth. Twice the United States has been confronted with the problem of how to act in the event of a war of wide dimensions outside the American continent. Twice it has been reluctant to enter the struggle. Twice it has finally done so. Does not this clearly show that it is better for the American government to combine with others for the maintenance of peace, rather than to interpose after war has broken out, and after it stands in increasing peril from the standpoint of its own security?

Such, at any rate, has been the reasoning of those responsible for American policy since 1945. The constant iteration of the doctrine of collective security has played a substantial part in altering the American point of view. It has led to the adoption of a series of alliances which form the basis of American policy today.

There was some realization at San Francisco of the fact that regional and partial agreements might offer more hope of peace than did universal covenants. The Charter expressly sanctions such agreements and today the United States, which for so long scrupulously avoided "entanglements," has agreements with many, many countries in numerous parts of the world. We should examine these agreements and ask what is their utility in the effort to attain peace.

First of all, let me say again that the very existence of these alliances marks hardly less than a revolution in the foreign policy of the United States. It is not merely that they are unprecedented. The important thing to note is that in them, implicitly or explicitly, is the recognition of the fact that physical power is an element in the maintenance of peace. The point can hardly be overemphasized. Throughout their history, in their search for peace, Americans have tended to depreciate the role of force. But you can no more separate power from politics than you can separate sex from marriage. You can sublimate power, as you can sublimate sex. But you cannot exorcise it. To the degree that we in this country have come to recognize this fact, we may have made progress in the search for a more ordered world.

The engagements of the United States today extend over a wide field. There is, for example, the North Atlantic Treaty Organization, which provides for the defense of Europe, and of which, besides a substantial number of European states, Turkey is a member. There is the so-called Treaty of Manila, which provides for the security of a number of states in the Far East. There are separate commitments to the Philippines, to Nationalist China, to Korea, and to Japan. There is the so-called Rio Protocol, which concerns the area of Latin America. How are these various alliances to be evaluated? What are their terms? How great is their internal solidity? How effective are they likely to be in the preservation of peace?

This last question we cannot answer categorically. We can say that in none of the areas touched by these treaties has there been an attack against the states which have made them—with one exception. We can argue, therefore, that their deterrent effect has been substantial. But since we cannot with precision plumb the purposes of the possible aggressors, we must not say too positively that they have prevented war. There is a strong likelihood, in certain areas, that this is so. But there is no certainty.

Of the various pacts we have mentioned, by far the most important is the North Atlantic Pact. This pact was signed in 1949. It came about in riposte to Russian action in Eastern Europe, to the subversion of democracy in Czechoslovakia, to the attempt to squeeze the occupying powers out of Berlin, and to the establishment of Russian military control over the states of Eastern Europe. The parties to the pact agreed to develop their capacity to resist armed attack "by means of continuous and effective self-help and mutual aid." Article 5 stipulated that an armed attack upon any one of them would be regarded as an attack upon all, and that each would render assistance to the aggressed power "by such action as it deems necessary, including the use of armed force." This engagement was ratified by the Senate of the United States by the impressive vote of 82 to 13.

Any alliance is subject to centrifugal tendencies. There may be a change of government in one of the states concerned which leads to its withdrawal from the alliance itself; there may be dragging of the feet in connection with the operation of the agreement; there may be a lack of resolution when the decisive moment comes. Indeed, it would be strange if perfect harmony existed among allies. We must expect some measure of disagreement; but the greater the external pressure the less the disagreement will be and the better the prospect that the alliance will stand the strain.

Insofar as the decay of the alliance from within is concerned, that is, decay through actual subversion, or from the establishment of a pro-Communist regime in any Western European state, we have little to fear. Europe, thanks in no small part to the statesmanship of the Marshall Plan, has staged a sensational recovery since 1945; the internal strength of the Communist movement has been undermined by prosperity; Socialism itself, in any precise sense of the word, is a declining force; and the sentiment of national independence furnishes a powerful reinforcement to the forces of cohesion. Western Europe, no doubt, is still far from that federation of which some Americans like to dream but it is nearer to the constitution of an international community than it has ever been in the past.

At the same time NATO has been subjected to very substantial strain; its level of forces is not what was originally planned; the French have withdrawn a large part of their military contingents to carry on the war in

[83]

Algeria and they are putting forward demands for a more decisive and central role in the operation of the alliance, demands which it is difficult to meet. There exists in other countries a feeling that the danger of attack by the Soviet Union is not very great and therefore some reluctance to make sacrifices for the national defense. But in the discussion of the question of Berlin, the allies have declared that they would oppose any unilateral alteration of the status of that city by any means, including nuclear power, and it is reasonably certain that in the event of a direct invasion of the West by the Soviet Union, the North Atlantic pact would stand the strain. We must, on balance, consider it a major fact in the promotion of peace and the maintenance of stability as matters stand today. No one seriously proposes its dissolution.

Let us look next at our various alliances in the Far East. We have, for example, a treaty of defense with the Republic of South Korea. This treaty appears to have been effective in preventing any resumption of hostilities in that area. The South Korean army has been effectively reconstituted; behind it stands the power of the United States; and the Chinese Communists, despite their bad faith in the observance of the armistice, have either not dared, or not desired, to challenge the situation in that quarter.

We have a treaty with the Nationalist government on the island of Formosa. By this treaty the parties agree to regard an attack on the territory of either of them as dangerous to the peace and safety of both, and "to act to meet the common danger in accordance with their constitutional processes." This treaty had the overwhelming support of the Senate of the United States. Its practical effect has been to restrain the government of General Chiang Kai-shek from military adventure; at the same time it has, presumably, done something to discourage the Communists. In 1957 the Peiping government attempted to sound out the situation by launching an attack on the islands of Quemoy and Matsu, which were not explicitly covered by the treaty of 1954. They were successfully opposed by the government on Formosa but they might have pressed the situation further if there had not been in Washington clear intimations that all-out hostilities might involve the United States.

Of substantial significance is the so-called Treaty of Manila. This treaty was signed by the Philippines, Thailand, Pakistan, Great Britain, France, Australia, New Zealand, and the United States. It declares that an attack on any one of them would be regarded as dangerous to the peace and safety of the others. Each signatory agrees to "act to meet the common danger in

[85]

accordance with its constitutional processes." Here again there has been no such testing as affords a judgment as to the value of the association.

There is also an agreement with Japan, by which we maintain forces in the islands, as a deterrent to aggression, and there is an agreement with South Vietnam, by which we have strengthened there the anti-Communist regime of Ngo Dinh Diem.

Taking all these agreements together, it is reasonable to regard them as a barrier to Communist aggression. They have, so far as we can see, tended to stabilize the situation in the Far East.

There is a reasonable question that can be raised in connection with our various political associations in the Far East. The danger, it may be contended, does not consist in direct aggression. It consists in the subversion of existing governments. Alliances, it is contended, can be no protection against this danger. The point has significance. An attempt was made to deal with it in the Treaty of Manila, which provides for consultation and collective action in case of subversive activity. But it is true, none the less, that the machinery of an alliance offers a very inadequate guarantee against an internal revolution. Such a revolution can often be carried out with the forms of law. Interference with it can be labeled an act of intervention in the affairs of an independent state; it can rouse the sentiment of nationalistic resistance; and even if successful, it can seem to justify the accusation of imperialism, a deadly accusation in the world of today.

The deduction which many persons draw from this is that the true policy in the less advanced parts of the world is a policy of economic assistance, which, by improving the status of individuals, will make violent change less likely. There is some force in this point of view. The case runs for, and not against, economic aid, if stated in broad terms. But there are two qualifications that have to be made. Revolutions sometimes occur in populations which, having improved their economic position, are impatient to improve it still more. And it is also true that where aid is given safeguards have to be erected to provide for its wise use, and such safeguards are often obnoxious to the sensitive pride of the peoples concerned.

But let us return to our alliances. The Rio pact of 1947, the earliest in point of time, regulates our relationships with the states of Latin America. By its terms, the American states bind themselves to come to the assistance of an attacked state, the nature of the action to be determined by a two-thirds vote of the members of the alliance. In this case, therefore, the United States may be bound to take action with which it is not in

[87]

sympathy. It is provided, however, that this obligation does not apply to the use of armed force.

What shall we say of this alliance? Having in mind that the whole alliance system is directed against the Russians and the Chinese Communists, it seems unlikely that the occasion to invoke the terms of the Rio Protocol will be applied. It is more probable that the Kremlin would employ the technique of subversion, as was the case in Guatemala a few years ago. Here the non-intervention doctrine, to which the United States has committed itself more than once, might create an embarrassing situation for the American government. Still, the pact would have its uses in case of a war between the United States and the Soviet Union. It would align the other states of the New World on our side. It might result in the severance of economic relations with the Moscow government. Its preventative value is small, however.

There is a fourth area in which the United States participated in the forming of an alliance, that is, in the Middle East. Here it smiled on, though it did not join, the Baghdad pact by which Turkey, Iran, Iraq, and Pakistan joined together for mutual defense. This agreement had unhappy consequences. The American engagement to Pakistan affronted Indian opinion, naturally enough. And the revolution in Iraq in 1958 ruptured the fabric of the pact in striking degree. Effective defense measures, in this area, in response to direct aggression, would seem extraordinarily difficult. Moreover, it is likely that here, as in some other areas, the means of aggression would be by subversion rather than by direct attack and the same difficulties in dealing with subversion are present that are present in some other areas of the world.

We come now to the end of our brief analysis of the system of alliances that the United States has built up since the end of the war. We have seen that these alliances vary in their terms. We have seen that they provide no answer to the problem of Communist subversion. We have seen that it cannot be mathematically demonstrated that they have served as preservers of peace. Yet we can ask one central question, and make one central generalization. The question is: Is it not likely that, in the absence of such agglomeration of power, the policies of the Soviet Union and of the Chinese People's Republic would have been more aggressive than they have been? The generalization is that, without knowing it, the American people and the American government have accepted the principle of the balance of power as an instrument of peace. Many Americans do not wish to be told this. Yet the facts are clear.

Such a prescription for the maintenance of international tranquillity, however, is far from satisfying. *Any* balance is precarious. It may be eroded. It may involve constant and costly competition between those on one side and those on the other. Moreover, the balance in our own day involves an entirely new element. It involves the question of nuclear war. The attempt to maintain the balance does not guarantee peace; it may lead to a large-scale conflict involving destruction on a scale hitherto unknown. Or conversely, the perils involved in maintaining it may lead to a weakening of the national will, to the feeling that anything is better than nuclear war, and that any concession is better than nuclear catastrophe. In such a situation is there any way to bring about a more stable situation? An answer frequently put forward is that the way out of our present situation is through drastic measures of disarmament. What does the experience of the past suggest as to this proposal? What does the present posture of affairs suggest? To these questions I shall turn in my final chapter.

## 3

# Peace through Disarmament

IN THEIR SEARCH FOR THE PRESERVATION
of peace, the American people through their government have turned in recent years to the policy of alliance with other powers dedicated to the same end. The
public opinion of the nation is behind this policy—
witness the overwhelming votes by which most of these
treaties were ratified, and the bipartisan support which
they command in the Congress of the United States.
Such a policy has meant the building up of great armaments, such as the United States has never had before.
It has meant assistance to other nations in the strengthening of their military forces. And, while its necessity

seems to be widely, if not universally, admitted, it creates so many problems that, even in those who approve it, there is some sense of malaise, some uneasy feeling that there must be a better way. Many Americans have thought that a way might be found in the reduction of armaments. What does experience show in this regard?

Down to 1920, the interest shown by the American government in disarmament was tepid. True, there is the extraordinary agreement for the limitation of armaments on the Great Lakes going back to 1817; but this agreement stands alone. In the two Hague conferences the United States took a very reserved position on the whole question; its delegates seemed to stress the possible necessity for building up, rather than reducing, American physical power. It was only with the end of the First World War that the question of limiting armaments began to assume substantial importance. There were several reasons why, at this time, it should be brought to the fore. In the background of the war years was a growing naval competition between the United States and Japan. Both powers had been building on an increasing scale, and each was apprehensive of the other. At the same time it was official American policy to maintain a navy equal to that of Britain. This aspiration, too, might lead to competitive building. In such circumstances would not the limitation of armaments be in the long-run interest of the United States? Would it not relieve the American people of a substantial economic burden? Would it not improve the international atmosphere? These were reasonable questions, and they found their response in the resolution introduced by Senator Borah in the fall of 1920, requesting the President of the United States to call a conference for the restriction of naval forces. This resolution passed the Senate unanimously. The result was the conference of Washington, which first assembled on November 12, 1921.

I shall not examine the story of the conference in detail, though few diplomatic episodes are more interesting and dramatic. At the very opening of the conference Secretary Charles Evans Hughes held the center of the stage with a concrete proposal for naval limitation, and his proposals, after some modifications and much discussion, formed the basis for the agreement that was finally reached. At the conclusion of the meetings an agreement was signed regulating the number of battleships and aircraft carriers that might be maintained by the great powers, by France and Italy as well as by Great Britain, Japan, and the United States.

In coming to an agreement Secretary Hughes was much assisted by the strategy that he adopted, and by the climate of opinion in which he operated. He began with the assumption that existing ratios were to be maintained. Such an assumption was acceptable in the climate of 1921. Memories of the First World War were still young, and no nation was ready at the moment frankly to state that it was out to improve its naval position by outbuilding the others. The economic pressures making for peace in Japan, as well as in Britain and the United States, were substantial. The creation of the League of Nations, the meeting of the First League Assembly, the debate over the Covenant in the United States, all did something to stimulate a wave of peace sentiment. If the timing of a given policy is thought to be important, then the Washington conference of 1921 came at just the right moment.

Yet still it was necessary for Hughes to make important concessions to attain his end. The Japanese accepted the naval ratio proposed, that is three units to the American and British five, only after a formal agreement with the United States and Great Britain limiting the extension of fortifications in the Far East on the part of the last two powers. In other words, they demanded a guarantee of their own security in the Orient before they would limit their building. Putting the matter still more bluntly, they demanded a sphere of influence in which they would be exempt from the physical pressure of the Western powers. What they demanded they got.

There was something else on which Hughes had to yield. His proposals to base armaments on existing ratios stirred the sensitive pride of the French. In order to propitiate them, it was necessary to depart from the formula; and since the Italians demanded parity with the French, it was necessary to abandon the formula not once, but twice. Considerations of national pride took precedence over the rules of logic.

None the less, the agreement of 1922 (the treaty was actually signed in February of that year) was one of the most significant agreements ever reached in the field of armaments. Is it possible to draw any useful generalizations from the conference of 1922? I believe so. Let us see what conditions made possible the agreement in 1922.

The first condition was that an enormous sentiment in favor of peace had been generated by preceding events. The world had gone through a great war; in many of the most powerful nations the loss of life had been terrific; the madness of physical conflict had been starkly dramatized. The climate of world opinion was favorable to positive measures for reducing the tension between the nations.

In the second place, it was clear to the great powers

that entered into the agreements of Washington that the alternative to an understanding was an arms race. This fact is of the utmost importance. For, in order to limit armaments, there must be a widespread belief that the alternative is a bitter and protracted competition. If such a belief does not exist, the temptation on the part of one power to outbuild the other, and thus improve its relative position, is almost sure to be too strong to resist. This is another way of saying that any arms agreement must be, like most diplomatic transactions, the result of bargaining, and that the worst possible prelude to such bargaining is to make it clear that you do not really intend to meet the competitive challenge. This may seem a truism; yet many friends of disarmament overlook this essential fact, and by the very intensity of their interest and the pressure they seek to exert on their government they weaken its position in negotiation.

In the third place, the success of the Washington arms conference was due to the economic climate, and to the economic pressure felt by *all* the chief negotiating powers. One of the reasons why the British and the Germans could not agree on any slowing down of their naval programs in the years just before the First World War was that the Germans were feeling their economic oats; one of the reasons why the great powers did agree in 1922 was that each of them, after years of war, genuinely wished a period of economic tranquillity, a return to normalcy, as President Harding put it.

In the fourth place, agreement was possible in 1922 because the question of reducing armaments was related to the problem of security. We must see clearly that the price the Japanese got for "going along" was a virtual guarantee of immunity from attack in the Far East. To put the matter another way, the arms agreement carried with it political implications. To all intents and purposes the United States abdicated in the Orient, so far as the exercise of its physical power was concerned.

In the fifth place, success was made easier at Washington by the fact that only a small number of powers was concerned. Yet even with only five powers participating, there were difficulties. The French bucked like steers on the principle of existing ratios. It was necessary for Mr. Hughes to make a personal appeal to the French Premier, M. Briand, to get them to go along; it was necessary to stretch the principle of existing strength before they agreed to a treaty; and when they made a fuss the Italians followed suit. Is it not easy to see that had there been twenty naval powers instead of five, the problem would have been infinitely more difficult?

In the sixth place, in a naval agreement there was no very difficult question of controls. It was obviously a little difficult to build a battleship or an aircraft carrier clandestinely. It was wholly unnecessary to establish an elaborate system of supervision to see that the agreement was observed in practice.

Lastly, understanding was possible because the participating states seriously doubted whether any useful purpose was to be served by increasing the number of the types of vessels which they limited. The role of the battleship was a matter of debate. The importance of the aircraft carrier was not as yet fully envisaged. The pressures for reduction of armaments were thus satisfied in a limited area, and in an area where the problem perhaps was easiest.

We need deal only briefly with the naval conference of 1930. Though at this conference there was an agreement to limit all types of naval vessels, the agreement was accepted only by the United States, Great Britain, and Japan. The French put in claims for increased tonnage, and the Italians again claimed parity with the French. Moreover, the limited accord that was reached involved *more* building by the United States and Japan in order to come to an agreed position in relation to Great Britain. Even as it was, the eventuating treaty met with violent opposition in Nippon. It was ratified by the Tokyo government only after the greatest difficulties, including the attempted assassination of the Japanese Prime Minister, and it was denounced by Japan in 1934.

In the year just mentioned the whole concept of naval limitation broke down, and increased building by Japan produced a totally new situation. Why did it break down, and is there anything to be learned from the circumstances of the breakdown? I am inclined to think that there is. In the thirties the world was suffering from the most serious economic depression in history. The depression had one of two effects: in some countries it produced an extreme indifference to problems of foreign policy, an unwillingness to take risks, a tendency to avoid difficult decisions; in others it undeniably gave rise to an intransigent and bitter nationalism. From these facts I deduce a general principle. Closely connected with the problem of international tranquillity is that of the intelligent management of the economic order. In proportion as the nations of the world learn to deal wisely with questions of monetary management and economic health, the tension in international affairs may perhaps be lessened. I believe that some progress has been made along this line.

Let us turn from the question of naval armaments to the question of land armaments. In the discussion of this question in the 1920's and 1930's the United States necessarily played a subordinate role. Its own military forces were extraordinarily small, only about 130,000. The central problem was a European problem, and it is to be remembered that the Covenant of the League of Nations pledged the contracting parties to action in this regard. Article VIII stipulated that "the maintenance of peace requires the reduction of national armaments to the lowest point consistent with domestic safety." It was in accordance with this engagement that the League set up what was called the Preparatory Commission on Disarmament in 1925, and after years of negotiation called a Disarmament Conference in 1932. In these discussions the United States participated, and while, as I have just said, its role was not a central one, there is much to be learned from the deliberations in which it took part. To put the matter in a few words, these deliberations failed. Why?

We have seen that one of the conditions for the success of the Washington arms conference was the moral and economic climate. A long and bloody war had just ended. The sacrifices of that war were fresh in the mind. The costs of that war were no less fresh. But in 1932 the conditions were essentially different. The world depression had produced an outburst of violent nationalism. In Germany that sinister man, Adolf

Hitler, was on his way to power. In France apprehension as to the revival of Germany was widespread. There could hardly have been conditions less favorable for a cool discussion of the question of armaments.

In 1922 an agreement was reached by basing the settlement on the *status quo,* with due regard for the security of the various parties to the agreement. In 1932 what was being discussed was an alteration of the *status quo.* By the treaty of Versailles Germany had been disarmed. She was now clamoring for release from the unilateral obligations that she had then assumed. But the French, very naturally, and very rightly, as the events proved, feared the consequences of such a release. They had built up since 1919 a series of alliances with other states on the Continent by which their own position had been strengthened. They had maintained substantial military forces while Germany remained disarmed. They were unwilling to make any drastic reductions in their own strength, or to permit an increase in the strength of Germany, unless assured of more effective support against aggression than was accorded by the Covenant of the League. In particular, they sought some additional commitment from the United States. Such support the United States was unwilling to give. It made it clear from the beginning of the discussion that it could undertake no obligation to cooperate with the members of the League either in the form of military or economic pressure against an aggressor nation. This attitude made agreement unlikely. While we cannot say with certainty that a contrary view would have made an accord possible, we must, I think, in retrospect, regret the position of the American government.

But apart from these considerations, land disarmament was a far more difficult problem than naval disarmament. The Russians, who participated in the conference, did not seem much bothered by this. Then, as today, they brought forward a proposal for general and total disarmament. One may doubt that their motive was sincere. "The aim of the Soviet proposals," as stated in a Resolution of the Sixth World Congress of the Communist International, "is not to spread pacifist illusions, but to destroy them; not to support capitalism by ignoring or toning down its shady sides, but to propagate the fundamental Marxian postulate, that disarmament and the abolition of war are possible only with the fall of capitalism." It goes without saying that not a single Communist thought for a moment that the imperialists would accept the Soviet disarmament proposals. As today, no one at Geneva in 1932 took the sweeping Russian proposals seriously. But more limited proposals met with insuperable difficulties. We need not dwell on the fact that at Geneva it was not a question of a few nations, but of a larger number of nations, coming to an agreement. But we must emphasize the immense complexity of the problem of regulating land armaments as compared with the problem of agreeing on naval ratios.

On the side of land armaments, for example, a vexed question was that of reserves. The countries which had small professional armies based on long-term enlistment naturally believed in comparing their forces with those of nations which had reserves. These reserves should be taken into account in providing for any reduction on a proportionate basis. The countries which had conscription, on the other hand, took the view that only the forces actually in being should be counted. The latter position was maintained with particular tenacity by the French. For a long time the British and the Americans resisted this stand, but by 1929 the French had won the argument. But now the Germans dissented violently, and it was therefore evident that, while the three Western powers had decided to stand together, they would have much difficulty in imposing their views, and in writing them into a draft convention.

A still more difficult question was the question of the limitation of war material. The number of weapons used in land warfare was almost infinitely various. How would it be possible to regulate all of them? How would it be possible to undertake successfully the herculean task of describing and classifying them? How to see to it that none of the numerous governments involved violated its agreements?

The Preparatory Commission wrestled long with this problem. One way of answering it was to ban a substantial number of weapons, thus reducing the number to be regulated, and especially to ban the more dangerous weapons. Another way of dealing with the problem —at least in part—was to find some means of supervision.

The first of these answers came up in many forms, but was never very satisfactorily answered. An attempt was made to draw a distinction between offensive and defensive weapons. The Americans contended that if the truly offensive weapons were limited the fear of war would be lifted, and the way to substantial success in reducing armaments would be assured. But it proved in practice virtually impossible to draw this distinction. To the Americans and the British, for example, the submarine was an offensive weapon, the viper of the seas. To the French, on the other hand, it appeared as of purely defensive importance. At the conference of 1932, to take another example, protracted argument took place as to when artillery was defensive, and when it was offensive. If its caliber was 107 was it defensive; if it was 210 was it offensive? And what about the calibers in between? How distinguish between airplanes? When were they defensive, and when were they offensive? What about tanks? To the British small tanks seemed purely defensive, though to some other powers this was nonsense. What about aircraft carriers? With a total lack of humor, the American delegation had the effrontery to argue in the presence of the Japanese that aircraft carriers were purely defensive, although the only way the American forces could get at the Japanese was through the carrier. To put the matter bluntly, as the authors of *The United States in World Affairs for 1932* declared, "Every conceivable type of weapon was eulogized by some delegation as being in all respects defensive." It might be added that almost invariably the weapon so eulogized was possessed in quantity by the power that did the eulogizing.

With regard to the regulation of material, another difficulty suggested itself. This was the difficulty of qualitative as distinguished from quantitative limitation. This difficulty had been revealed in the naval agreement of 1922. Under that compact, cruisers were to be limited to 10,000 tons. But under a similar limitation imposed by the treaty of Versailles the Germans had constructed a cruiser, which, from the angle of effectiveness in battle, was believed to be far stronger than any of those possessed by the other naval powers. If quantitative measures could be evaded in the field of naval vessels, how much more likely was it that human ingenuity would find a way to evade such requirements in the vast and complex field of military weapons?

But granted that these difficult and delicate questions could be solved, what would be the machinery by which an agreement for the limitation of arms would be enforced? We have seen that, in the case of the treaty of Washington, the answer to this problem was simple. But it was certainly not simple in the case of land armaments.

One possible way of dealing with the problem was to set budgetary limits on the armed strength of the various states. At the outset the United States opposed his idea unequivocally. As a nation with high armament costs, it was quite unwilling to submit to this type of control. The original proposal had to be modified. The next step was to propose, not fixed limitation, which with price variations and variations in wages was clearly impracticable, but a comparison of annual budgets with some allowance for these variable factors. This, too, was for a time resisted by the United States. By 1932 the American government had again modified

its stand, but no acceptable formula had been dis-
covered.

Still a third expedient was suggested to make sure
that engagements, once taken, would be observed. This
was the establishment of a Permanent Disarmament
Commission, with supervisory powers. From the beginning the French insisted on this principle, declaring
that any agreement "would be absolutely useless unless
some means of enforcement or supervision were instituted in one form or another." The United States at
first opposed this point of view, declaring (here one
thinks of the Soviet Union of a not so remote period)
that such supervision was objectionable in principle,
and "contrary to the conception of good faith as the
foundation of international agreements." But with time
this view was modified, and provision was made for
a Commission which should "examine and judge the
information supplied by the signatories, to watch the
application of the projected treaty, and report regularly
on it." This, however, was only an agreement in principle. Neither the Preparatory Commission, nor the
Geneva Conference itself, was able to go beyond this
point. It seems right to say that it was a feeble step indeed toward the necessary end.

The difficulties of disarmament were dramatically
and vividly indicated when, in an effort to bring the

long discussions to some fruitful end, President Hoover electrified the Geneva Conference with a series of concrete proposals in June of 1932. The President proposed a reduction of one-third in the strength of land armies, over and above a police component, which was fixed at 100,000 troops for every 65,000,000 people, with some allowance, not defined, to be made for powers "having colonial possessions." Hoover also proposed the abolition of all tanks, all large mobile guns, all bombing planes, all instruments of chemical warfare, and substantial reductions in naval tonnage. This ambitious program, like so many others, was applauded and then opposed.

The American plan identified the United States with the revisionist forces in Europe—with renascent Germany. When the American government attempted to modify it, to satisfy the British and the French, more resentment was aroused. Finally, with an irony that was bitter indeed, the American delegation at the conference had to vote against its original proposals, in order to propitiate the French and the British. The Hoover plan, hailed enthusiastically when it was first presented, ended as a fiasco.

I do not intend to follow the Geneva conference through its various phases until it finally collapsed. After the accession of Hitler to power in Germany in

January 1933, there was not the slightest chance that anything would come of it. Indeed, in the spring of that year Germany withdrew from the League of Nations. The points that should stick in our minds when we look back to 1932 and the preceding years are these. First, any far-reaching scheme of disarmament presents and will present a great many complications and a great many hurdles. Second, it must take due account of the security needs of all the major powers. Thirdly, it must be presented at a time of relatively relaxed tension, and must not involve a sharp shift in the balance of military power.

You cannot expect one nation, or a group of nations, to give up its pre-eminent position, and you cannot expect another nation or group of nations not to strive for equality.

We come next to the remarkable story of the middle forties. It will always be to the credit of the United States that at the end of the war, after the dropping of the bomb, and at a moment when it held a clear ascendancy in the atomic field, it was ready to come forward with a plan for the limitation and internationalization of atomic power as an instrument of war. The plan is usually known as the Acheson-Lilienthal-Baruch plan. On the 14th of June, 1946, Bernard Baruch presented this plan to the Atomic Energy Commission set up by the United Nations. It called for the establishment of an International Atomic Development Authority. This authority was to have exclusive control of the production of world supplies of uranium and thorium. It was to sell these supplies, but only in denatured form, to individual nations. It was to carry on research in atomic explosives, dispersing its plants, facilities, and stock piles in such a way that they could not be situated within any one nation, or any small group of nations. Any activities carried on outside it were to be regarded as illegal, and might call for punitive action on the part of the United Nations. In determining what action should be taken against a violator, the Security Council, as the authoritative body of the United Nations, was to decide on the necessary steps, and its action was not to be subject to the veto.

This grandiose plan came to nothing. It went so far that it might in any case have been difficult to reduce it to an international agreement which would receive general international adhesion. But it was received very coldly indeed by the representative of the Soviet Union. The details of the controversy which arose are difficult to follow, and the Russians, as so often, sought to muddle the issue by all sorts of shifts in the debate in the Commission. They insisted upon an agreement for the abolition of all atomic weapons before they would consent to discuss a plan for an international authority. In other words, they seemed to require that the United States divest itself of its advantage in the world of power before they would agree to any system of inspection, or to any international control. The discussion was long and confused; at a given moment the representative of the Soviet Union seemed to indicate that day-to-day supervision by the Authority might be conceded; but he never wavered in the contention that punitive action against a violator would be subject to the veto. Whatever else may be said on the question, it seems clear that the possibilities of an agreement progressively deteriorated as the tension between the Soviet Union and the United States increased. Stating the matter as objectively as possible, the American government had made a great and magnanimous gesture; there is little evidence that it was met in the same spirit.

It was the same with more general proposals for the reduction of armaments. In 1946 and 1947 the matter was discussed at length in the Security Council. At times the Russians seemed to be making concessions. The key question, as in earlier conferences, was the question of inspection. While the Russian delegation at times paid lip service to the principle, they seem never to have gotten down to brass tacks on the matter. It does not seem unfair to say that they chose rather to build up their own armaments than to enter in good faith into an arrangement with the United States.

We come now to the present. What are the chances of disarmament today? To what degree may we hope for an accord on this field of endeavor? Is the experience of the past to be repeated, or may we look forward to a happier era? At a time when man's power of destruction is greater than ever before, will it be possible to recognize the portentous character of armament today, and find some way to limit it?

Before entering upon an analysis of the problem, I must frankly state that the idea of total disarmament is an iridescent dream. It seems hardly likely that Mr. Khrushchev is sincere in proposing it, any more than was Mr. Litvinov in 1927. The hollow nature of the Russian proposal is well demonstrated by the demand that the nations disarm first, and discuss the question of supervision afterward. It is further revealed by the fact that more concrete and limited proposals followed on the sweeping suggestions with which the Russian premier began.

In private, [writes William R. Frye of the *Christian Science Monitor* in the *Foreign Policy Bulletin* of the Foreign Policy Association for October 15, 1959] no seasoned diplomat here takes the Khrushchev total disarmament proposal seriously. It is the butt of quips about baseball bats and kitchen knives, "the weapon of the future." Even the Russians seem to have a hard time keeping a straight face when they talk about the plan. None of this feeling, however, is being allowed to come to the surface. If the West could be maneuvered into the position of scoffing at the Khrushchev plan, or rejecting it out of hand, the Soviet Union would be put in the role of peacemaker and the West in the position of peace opponent, so far as a large segment of world opinion is concerned. And if Khrushchev could persuade the world that he is Mr. Peace in person just by offering a plan for total disarmament, there would be no need for him to make genuine concessions to win that title. It would be the West which would be under pressure to match his magnanimity.

Let us, then, abstain from all illusions as to the early dawn of an armament Utopia.

But can some kind of limited progress be made? In particular, can an agreement in the field of nuclear testing be arrived at? The situation, as this book goes to press, is fluid, and I can do no more than indicate some of the elements in the problem.

Negotiations on the suspension of testing have now been going on between the three nuclear powers for more than two years. They have turned particularly on the matter of inspection, and there have been occasions when it seemed as if an accord might be reached. The spread of nuclear weapons to other powers constitutes an obvious danger to the states that now possess them. The resumption of testing, and the further proliferation of nuclear armaments, would constitute a heavy burden on the economies of Great Britain, the Soviet Union, and the United States. The dread of nuclear war is a force that makes for agreement, whether logically or not.

On the other hand, the inspection question has not been solved, and of late the Russians have put forward an absurd and inadmissible demand for a kind of veto on inspection proceedings. Moreover, suspension is meaningful only if it is accepted by all the powers. Is it at all certain that if Russia, the United States, and Great Britain came to an agreement, the other nations of the world would follow? How about the Chinese, now in a fiercely nationalistic mood? How about the French, who appear determined to seek membership in the nuclear club? It would be foolish, as matters stand, to answer these questions, and particularly foolish to assume that the attitude of these states did not constitute a difficult problem.

In any case, let us not exaggerate the importance of an agreement on nuclear testing, as a solution of the problem of international relations. If success comes, there will still be great stockpiles in existence in both Russia and the United States, and these stockpiles may be increased. The competition of armaments between the two great countries will have been attenuated, but it will not have ceased. It will still be vitally necessary to maintain a defense posture which, in every essential respect, is capable of containing the power of the Soviet Union. I return to this question a little later.

One more point. An agreement on nuclear testing is more likely, of course, if there is some relaxation in the political atmosphere. One cannot, as I write, be optimistic on this point. Russian policy consists of verbal blandishments and irritating action. But some hope exists, none the less.

I will deal only cursorily with other possible proposals for the control of armaments. Some agreement might be reached on the prevention of surprise attack. Such an agreement would certainly do something to diminish tension. President Eisenhower, in fact, has proposed an understanding on this point and since it is in the interest of all states to prevent such an attack, a bilateral agreement might be extended, perhaps, without too much difficulty. But so far the Russians have not responded.

Another line of approach to the nuclear problem is

the proposal for the establishment of a neutral or nuclear-free zone in Europe. It is difficult to make a judgment on a project of this kind unless it is spelled out in detail. At times, in supporting it, the Russians talk as if the precondition to such an accord was the elimination of all American bases in Europe, and the virtual break-up of the North Atlantic Treaty Organization. Such terms, of course, would be completely unacceptable to the United States. Whether a more limited agreement could be reached is a matter on which, at the moment, it is hardly possible to express a really informed opinion. I will only observe that if an agreement is to be reached, it must be one that takes into consideration the interest of our allies. Americans too frequenty talk as if all we had to do was to sit down with the Russians and come to an agreement. This is, most emphatically, not the case. When Khrushchev came to the United States, President Eisenhower very properly declined to enter into any binding commitments before consulting our associates. There is no other way to deal with this problem. And if we *do* so consult, we shall, of course, find some divergences of viewpoint. There is, therefore, no reason as yet to believe that a nuclear-free zone can be established. It will be some time before we can judge accurately the possibilities in this regard.

The analysis I have just made is, of necessity, of the moment. It may be refuted by events. But in two respects it can be of something more than negative value. It underlines the conditions under which an agreement on armaments is possible. It makes it clear, I hope, that success in this field is related to the general conditions which prevail when understanding is attempted.

If our hopes are in some degree realized in the ensuing months—or years—we must still evaluate correctly what is involved. Success will have a genuine and positive value. It will result, almost inevitably, in some relaxation of tension, in a better climate in which to deal with the more concrete questions which trouble our relations with the Soviet Union. But it will still leave great supplies of arms in being; it will not exorcise the possibility of nuclear war; it will not bring us very near to the millennium.

There is a central point that needs to be emphasized, in my judgment, in any summation of the problem. This central point is that the relationship of the great nations of the world is a power relationship, and will remain a power relationship for a long time to come. Unless we understand this clearly, we cannot begin to deal with the international problem. Our first and fundamental principle must be to remain strong. If we do this, if we do not flinch in the maintenance of that power which is no less the deterrent to violence than a possible incitement to violence, we may conceivably win through to a new age. Some people tell us that armaments of themselves breed war. But the history of two decades ago demonstrates convincingly that weakness also breeds war. The melancholy history of the thirties should be in the minds of all of us. Intent on their own economic welfare, reluctant to make sacrifices, the Western powers neglected their defenses, and watched with complacency the balance of power shift against them. As it shifted, the wicked man who ruled Germany pushed further and further toward domination of the Continent. And finally, the worm turned, as, considering the character of the human being, it was bound to turn. When the choice became clearer and clearer between deep humiliation and war, the Western powers chose war, war at the worst possible moment, and under the worst possible conditions. And the United States? There may have been a time when decisive action by the American government could have given a different color to events. I said may, just may. If the United States had wholeheartedly supported the League of Nations, if it had encouraged instead of discouraged the Geneva Protocol, if it had not in the thirties pursued a narrowly isolationist course, it is just possible that the holocaust of the years 1939–45 might have been averted. Whether this is so or not, the history of the inter-war years affords ample evidence that indifference, unwillingness to sacrifice, constant submission before the advance of evil, is not a proper prescription for the maintenance of peace.

We must grasp this principle in its fullest extent. While abstaining from provocation, while making it crystal clear that we do not intend to change the *status quo* by force of arms, we must also make it clear that we will not permit it to be disturbed by others by measures of international violence. Nothing could be more unwise than for us to disseminate the idea that there is no aggression which we would not condone, no assault upon the liberties of others that we would not tolerate. One of the surest guarantees of peace would be a clear statement by the United States and its allies as to what it will resist in the international sphere. This was the doctrine of John Foster Dulles, the doctrine that by making clear one's intention to resist, one made violence less likely. This is what Winston Churchill meant when he said that in our time peace might be the sturdy child of terror.

It may be that we are on the threshold of a new age. It may be that we have made aggression so dangerous that it will not be attempted. It may be that so strong is the prepossession of the Soviet Union today for an improvement in the economic status of its people that no dangerous issue will arise in our intercourse with that power. It may be that we can set some bounds to the spread of nuclear armaments, and that the nuclear armaments which exist will constitute a powerful guarantee of peace. It may be that we shall see a great decrease in international tension in the years ahead. Surely we should not wring our hands in futility. Great winds of hope are sweeping through the world, the hope of peace, the hope of economic progress, of a richer life for all. This is no time for despair. It is a time for understanding, for wisdom, and for the forward view. To win through to a new order will require all the courage, and all the faith, and all the wisdom that we can command. Let it at least be said of us that we tried, that we have given what we have to give, that we have been equal to the challenge of our times.